ALBATROSS

C.W. STEINLE

ALBATROSS

Faith, Science, and the Future

C. W. Steinle

2025

Albatross: Faith, Science, and the Future
By C. W. Steinle

Copyright © 2025 by Memorial Crown Press
Phoenix, AZ, USA

ISBN: 979-8-9919337-3-5

Unless otherwise noted, scripture quotations in this book are taken from the ESV® Bible (The Holy Bible, English Standard Version®), © 2001 by Crossway, a publishing ministry of Good News Publishers. Used by permission. All rights reserved; and, the New King James Version. Copyright 1982 by Thomas Nelson, Inc. Used by permission. All rights reserved.

Ordering Information:
Special discounts are available on quantity purchases by corporations, associations, educators, and others. Contact the publisher or distributor for details.
info@memorialcrownpress.com

U.S. trade bookstores and wholesalers: Please contact the distributor.

ABOUT THE AUTHOR

C. W. Steinle is a Christian author and teacher whose work bridges faith, history, and science. With more than twenty-five books to his name, he is known for challenging popular assumptions about prophecy while opening new vistas for Christian thought. Steinle has taught on location in Israel, Greece, and Egypt, blending scholarship with lived experience. He lives in Phoenix, Arizona, with his wife, Gwen, where they share a passion for biblical studies and family life.

DEDICATION

Albatross broadens the Overton Window enabling an honest investigation of ancient faith and space age science. In the spirit of open discourse, this book is dedicated to the late Charlie Kirk.

PREFACE

WHY ALBATROSS?

The metaphor of "an albatross around one's neck" traces directly to Samuel Taylor Coleridge's 1798 poem *The Rime of the Ancient Mariner*. In this iconic work, a mariner inexplicably kills an albatross—a seabird long regarded in maritime folklore as a harbinger of good fortune and a guide through treacherous waters. Sailors had for centuries believed the albatross embodied the spirits of dead seafarers or divine messengers bringing favorable winds. To kill such a bird was thought to court disaster.

Coleridge dramatized this superstition vividly in lines 63-82 of the poem. (Note that, like "rime," "thorough" is an archaic spelling, which also maintains the cadence):

At length did cross an Albatross,
Thorough the fog it came;
As if it had been a Christian soul,
We hailed it in God's name.

ALBATROSS — *C.W. Steinle*

It ate the food it ne'er had eat,
And round and round it flew.
The ice did split with a thunder-fit;
The helmsman steered us through!

And a good south wind sprung up behind;
The Albatross did follow,
And every day, for food or play,
Came to the mariner's hollo!

In mist or cloud, on mast or shroud,
It perched for vespers nine;
Whiles all the night, through fog-smoke white,
Glimmered the white Moon-shine.'

'God save thee, ancient Mariner!
From the fiends, that plague thee thus!--
Why look'st thou so?'--With my cross-bow
I shot the ALBATROSS.

The mariner's senseless act brings a curse upon the
ship: the winds cease, the sun scorches, the crew
languishes in thirst—decrying the irony: "Water,
water, everywhere, nor any drop to drink." At first,
the crew supports the killing but as their suffering
deepens, they turn on the mariner; hanging the dead
albatross about his neck as a visible sign of his guilt
and the burden of their misfortune. The weight
remains until the mariner learns reverence for life,

blesses the sea creatures, and the albatross falls from his neck into the ocean, symbolizing forgiveness and redemption.

THE WEIGHT WE CARRY IN THE MODERN WORLD

The image quickly transcended Coleridge's poem. The phrase "albatross around one's neck" entered English idiom to mean a **heavy, inescapable burden**—often moral or psychological—that arises from one's actions or circumstances. Literature, political speeches, and journalism alike have employed it to describe:

- **Guilt or remorse** one cannot shake off.
- **Consequences** of past mistakes haunting the present.
- **Obstacles or responsibilities** that weigh down progress or happiness.

For instance, politicians speak of economic crises as "an albatross around the nation's neck," while novelists invoke it to portray characters haunted by regret or tragedy. The metaphor resonates spiritually as well. The mariner's journey echoes themes of **sin, repentance, and redemption** familiar in Christian thought.

ALBATROSS — *C.W. Steinle*

The albatross becomes a cross-like burden, borne until the sinner experiences repentance followed by grace. Psychologically, it parallels the concept of carrying **emotional or existential weight**—the invisible loads of guilt, anxiety, or regret; which people often carry like baggage throughout their lives.

Today, the expression applies far beyond seafaring or poetry. Corporate scandals become "albatrosses" for companies; personal regrets become "albatrosses" in memoirs; failed policies linger as "albatrosses" in political commentary. Its durability stems from the powerful mental picture Coleridge created: a once-living creature, now dead, hung—heavy and accusing—upon the shoulders of the guilty.

And so, an albatross has settled across space-age humankind's shoulders—a long, spectral thing. Its wings stretching from the fever of prophecy to the wonder of science, its weight pressing like judgment, like doubt, like division. It is the burden of apocalyptic resolve; even as the human spirit aches for the stars.

Mankind wondered if the true Race for Space was not truly against other nations—against distance, gravity, or time… but against the apocalyptic expectation that the physical skies themselves might soon close forever.

TABLE OF CONTENTS

PART I

THE ALBATROSS OF APOCALYPTIC FEAR

CHAPTER ONE
THE MAN BENEATH
TWO SKIES

The man stood beneath two skies...

One was the sky of prophecy—a storm-bruised horizon trembling with trumpet blasts and apocalyptic fire. In its shadowed expanse, voices whispered of wars and rumors of wars, of kingdoms toppling and stars falling. Preachers thundered of Israel reborn, of calendars ticking down toward the final day when history itself would bow before the returning Christ. This sky carried urgency like a fever, painting the world as a clock racing toward midnight.

The other sky was clear, infinite, unmarred by any sense of ending. It was the sky of rockets splitting clouds, of telescopes reaching for galaxies flung like jewels across the deep darkness of space. It beckoned with the hush of alien winds and the silence of untouched worlds waiting for human footprints.

This sky carried no prophecy of endings—only beginnings. It promised frontiers, civilizations yet unborn, the long adventure of humanity pressing outward into creation's uncharted parsecs.

But the man could not stand under both skies at once without feeling the weight. For the voices of one warned that the story was nearly over, while the other whispered that it had barely begun.

TWO GREAT EXPECTATIONS

It is here, in this moment of conflicting skies, that the twenty-first century finds itself. On one side, a dominant stream of Protestant eschatology looks backward to prophecies and forward to consummation, insisting that history now flails in its final hours. It points to the modern State of Israel, to Middle Eastern conflicts, to the shifting tides of global politics as proof that the end is at hand. Books, conferences, and entire movements have flourished around this sense of urgency. The faithful, in this view, are not so much preparing to inherit the earth as to escape from it.

On the other side, humanity faces outward with a spirit of discovery unmatched since the Age of Exploration. Telescopes reveal galaxies upon galaxies, an expanding universe so vast that even the most ambitious imaginations fall short. Space agencies plan colonies on the Moon and Mars. Private companies chart trajectories toward mining asteroids, terraforming planets, and carrying human life beyond the solar system itself.

Science fiction dares to write the opening pages of humanity's saga, as science fiction edges toward science fact. And torn between prophecy and possibility, between apocalypse and aspiration, stands modern man.

THE FIRST WEIGHT: DOOM AT THE DOOR

The problem lies not in prophecy itself, but in its psychological weight. For many Christians, the return of Christ looms so near, so inevitable, that long-term planning feels almost irrelevant. Why map the stars if heaven and earth are destined to pass away in our lifetime? Why reach for Mars if Christ will return before the first colony can take root?

This sense of imminence—rooted in scripture, yet often colored by sensationalism—has shaped entire generations. Every war, every earthquake, every political upheaval has been preached as a harbinger of the end. For some, this expectation fuels holiness and urgency in evangelism. For others, it fosters disengagement from the world, as though human achievement carries little weight in light of impending cosmic judgment.

Meanwhile, outside the Church, the world hears this, not as hope but as resignation. It sees faith not as a partner in progress but as a roadblock, a worldview chained to ancient prophecies rather than open to human possibility. The so-called "conflict between science and religion" often hides this deeper tension: a belief system awaiting its own conclusion set against a civilization yearning to explore the vastness of space.

Among the many weights humanity carries in the twenty-first century, few press as heavily on the shoulders of Christian thought as Protestant eschatology, particularly in its popularized, apocalyptic form. With the reestablishment of the modern State of Israel in 1948, millions of believers have been taught to read this event as a divine countdown clock, an eschatological trigger signaling the world's impending termination. Preachers and authors have made lucrative careers projecting timetables and warning of Christ's imminent return; while wars, famines, pandemics, and even technological advances are skillfully folded into this apocalyptic narrative as proof that the end is upon us.

Yet mankind stands at the edge of unprecedented exploration and discovery. Science is unraveling the genetic codes of life, peering into the deepest recesses of the cosmos, and sending its first emissaries beyond Earth's cradle. The human spirit of curiosity—the drive to expand, to build, to push boundaries—seems irrepressible. From the microchip to Mars rovers, from the mapping of the human genome to the search for habitable exoplanets, mankind stands poised at the edge of an era that could eclipse all prior ages of discovery.

And herein lies the tension. One worldview insists history is winding down toward an inevitable, divinely orchestrated conclusion; the other sees history as open-ended, waiting for human courage and intellect to chart its course among the stars. It is as though the human race is running two races at once: the apocalyptic sprint toward the finish line of time, and the exploratory marathon into virtually infinite space. Can there be parallels in these racetracks? Or, are they destined to collide?

THE PSYCHOLOGICAL AND SPIRITUAL IMPASSE

The eschatological "albatross" exerts subtle but profound pressure on both faith and science. On one side, some Christians hesitate to invest too deeply in the future—after all, why colonize Mars if Christ will return tomorrow? Why pour resources into curing disease or exploring interstellar travel if the heavens themselves are destined to "roll up like a scroll?" Much too often, and rightly so, secular scientists and explorers interpret this apocalyptic urgency as religious fatalism, a worldview that discourages progress and undermines humanity's responsibility to steward the earth and seek knowledge.

The result is a peculiar cultural and spiritual impasse:

- **For faith**: A focus on the imminent end can eclipse Christianity's broader call to cultivate wisdom, beauty, justice, and discovery—all expressions of the *imago Dei* (image of God).
- **For science**: The suspicion that religion opposes progress reinforces the "science versus faith" narrative, deepening division where there might be dialogue.

If this conflict persists, it risks hollowing out the Christian witness in a century when humanity most needs a faith robust enough to embrace both mystery and discovery.

COULD BOTH BE TRUE?

But perhaps the tension is false. Perhaps the skies do not contradict each other.

Christianity, at its heart, has always balanced paradox: the already and the not-yet, divine sovereignty and human freedom, eternity breaking into time, yet leaving history open for generations to flourish. Might Christ's return, then, be less about closing history down than about bringing it to fulfillment—whenever that may be?

If so, then humanity's urge to explore, to discover, to advance, need not stand in opposition to Christian hope. The cultural mandate given in Genesis—to fill the earth, to steward creation—may yet extend beyond Earth itself, calling mankind not merely to survive but to expand the boundaries of knowledge and habitation.

The question, then, is not whether Christ will return but whether Christians can embrace a vision of faith large enough to celebrate human progress without fear that it delays, diminishes, or competes with divine purposes.

TOWARD A THEOLOGY OF ONGOING CREATION

What if this is a false dilemma? What if Christ's eventual return does not negate humanity's call to explore, to build, and to press outward into creation's vast unknowns? Historically, Christian theology has spoken of the *cultural mandate*—the divine charge to "fill the earth and subdue it," to cultivate and extend human stewardship. Might the Space Age simply broaden that horizon beyond Earth itself?

The real "albatross" is not Christ's return but the narrow eschatological imagination that sees history only in terms of its ending rather than its unfolding purpose. Christianity has, in the past embraced enigmatic mysteries such as: God's transcendence yet ever-presence, human freedom yet divine sovereignty, the "already"—together with the "not-yet." Why should the relationship between Christ's return and humanity's future be any different?

10

A faith, mature enough to affirm both divine consummation *and* human discovery would free believers from paralyzing fear and free scientists from dismissing faith as anti-progress. It would encourage Christians to view the Space Age not as a futile race against God's clock but as part of the very story God is telling through humanity's quest for knowledge and dominion.

A PATH FORWARD

Such a perspective would:

1. **Relieve the existential burden**— removing the sense that faith demands disengagement from progress or suspicion toward science.

2. **Bridge the cultural divide**—showing that Christianity need not fear scientific advancement nor demand the immediate closure of history.

3. **Revitalize Christian hope**—not as escape from the world's story but as confidence that Christ's purposes encompass the fullness of history, however long it may unfold.

By disentangling the Gospel from rigid apocalyptic timetables, the Christian imagination could recover its sense of adventure, its intellectual vitality, its hope.

TOWARD A LARGER HOPE

To remove this "albatross" from humanity's shoulders is not to deny prophecy nor to abandon Christian hope. It is to free faith from the paralysis of immediacy—from the assumption that every scientific advance is without merit in God's eternal economy; merely a distraction from laying up treasure in heaven—a triviality that might even run contrary to God's plan.

A Christianity that is not detached from the physical future could inspire rather than hinder exploration. It could affirm that human discovery, far from challenging divine providence, unfolds under it—that the same God who made the stars also made minds capable of reaching for them.

Such a vision would relieve the existential burden pressing upon both believer and skeptic alike. It would allow faith to speak with confidence toward innovation rather than anxiety over the end of time, to bless rather than ignore or resist humanity's forward motion, to frame scientific progress as part of God's unfolding story rather than being a rival to His story.

Perhaps then, the man beneath the two skies could begin to lift his head—seeing not a contradiction but a calling, not an expiring hourglass but a horizon waiting to be crossed.

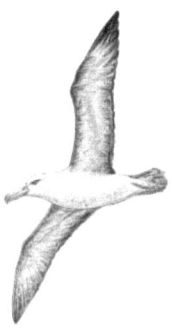

CHAPTER TWO
TRUMPETS, BEASTS, AND
BURNING STARS

How prophecy, politics, and popular theology converged to shape a generation's view of the end times.

The albatross that now hangs across the shoulders of modern Christianity did not descend in a single moment. It grew, decade by decade, out of sermons, marginal notes, world events, and an imagination fixed on the end rather than on the forward march of history. The burden feels inevitable now—as if Christians have always been looking at Israel, Russia, the Middle East, the United Nations, and the sky itself with apocalyptic suspicion. Yet this view of prophecy has a particular history, a modern one, shaped by nineteenth-century theology, twentieth-century geopolitics, and the cultural anxieties of a world at war with itself.

This chapter traces that story, the making of the albatross that has inhibited Christian engagement with science, discovery, and the future itself.

THE BIRTH OF MODERN ESCHATOLOGY

The roots reach back to the 1830s when John Nelson Darby, an Anglo-Irish preacher, divided biblical history into distinct "dispensations"— epochs in which God dealt with humanity in specific ways. One of Darby's boldest ideas was that the Church and Israel had separate destinies. Where older traditions saw Christianity as the spiritual fulfillment of Israel's story, Darby insisted Israel's national promises were still awaiting literal fulfillment—including its restoration to the land and the climactic events of the "end times."

Darby also popularized a teaching that would come to dominate twentieth-century evangelicalism: the *rapture*. According to this view, before a future period of tribulation and judgment, Christ would secretly remove his Church from the world, leaving unbelievers behind to face apocalyptic horrors.

At first, Darby's ideas spread among small circles in Britain and America. But in 1909, something happened that would change everything: the publication of the **Scofield Reference Bible**.

SCOFIELD'S MARGINS AND THE POWER OF PRINT

Cyrus I. Scofield, an American lawyer-turned-preacher, added extensive notes to the King James Bible explaining prophecy in Darby's terms. These footnotes declared, for example, that the rebirth of Israel would precede the second coming of Christ. For many readers, Scofield's notes carried as much authority as the biblical text itself.

And because his Bible appeared in the early twentieth century, at the height of America's mass-printing revolution, it spread far beyond seminaries and theologians. Ordinary churchgoers, Sunday school teachers, pastors, and missionaries began reading Scripture through Scofield's prophetic lens.

By the 1920s and 30s prophecy conferences filled halls across the United States. Charts depicting beasts from Daniel and trumpets from Revelation stretched across stages, drawing connections between modern events and ancient texts. A generation learned to view history as a divine countdown.

ISRAEL AND THE PROPHETIC IMAGINATION

Then came the real-world events that seemed to make those footnotes come alive.

- The Balfour Declaration of 1917—Britain's support for a Jewish homeland in Palestine—set prophecy teachers buzzing. Had God begun restoring Israel?
- The horrors of World War II and the Holocaust gave new urgency to the question.
- And then, in 1948, the modern State of Israel was born.

For many evangelicals, this was not merely politics; it was prophecy fulfilled before their eyes. Scofield's margins had spoken. Sermons rang out, *"This is the super-sign. The last days have begun."*

Israel became the prophetic clock, ticking toward Armageddon. Every Middle East war, every peace treaty, every rumor of conflict seemed to confirm it. The Cold War only deepened the sense of urgency—nuclear weapons and superpower tensions fit neatly into apocalyptic scripts.

THE AGE OF TIMETABLES AND BESTSELLERS

By the 1970s, prophecy teaching had moved from pulpits to paperbacks. Hal Lindsey's *The Late Great Planet Earth* sold millions, predicting that Israel's rebirth marked the final generation before Christ's return. He even suggested a date: within forty years of 1948. The math pointed to the 1980s. Lindsey's book became the best-selling nonfiction work of the decade. Youth groups watched end-times films like *A Thief in the Night*, where guillotines and Antichrist governments loomed large. Sermons warned believers never to plan too far ahead, college, careers—even families might be interrupted by the rapture.

Lindsey's work, selling over 35 million copies by the 1990s, epitomized Cold War apocalypticism, blending oil crises, nuclear proliferation, and Middle Eastern conflicts into premillennial dispensationalist frameworks popularized via Scofield's Reference Bible. Scholars of American religion[1] trace how such literature cemented a culture of prophetic immediacy shaping evangelical attitudes toward science, politics,

---

[1] Paul Boyer, *When Time Shall Be No More: Prophecy Belief in Modern American Culture* (Cambridge, MA: Harvard University Press, 1992).

19

and the future.[2] When 1988 came and went, prophecy teachers adjusted the numbers. Some claimed Israel's clock began in 1967, with the Six-Day War. Others insisted prophetic timeframes were symbolic. The dates changed; the sense of imminence did not.

Then came the *Left Behind* series in the 1990s and 2000s—apocalyptic thrillers selling over 80 million copies. For millions of readers, fiction shaped faith more than theology. The world's future was a set piece: rapture, tribulation, Armageddon, the end.

---

[2] Matthew Avery Sutton, *American Apocalypse: A History of Modern Evangelicalism* (Cambridge, MA: Harvard University Press, 2014).

CHAPTER THREE
THE WEIGHT OF THE CLOCK

For nearly two millennia, Western Christianity has carried a curious burden on its shoulders—a prophetic clock ticking in the background of faith.

It began with the apocalyptic imagery of Revelation and the messianic hope of early Judaism, then grew into a full theological framework: the world itself had a divinely appointed shelf life. Six thousand years for human history, followed by one thousand years of Christ's reign, then the end.

The implications were enormous. If the sands of time were slipping toward an imminent conclusion, then every famine, war, and eclipse seemed a cosmic signpost. As the centuries rolled on, this idea shaped Christian imagination: the future was not open but rapidly closing; history itself was running out of time.

FROM AUGUSTINE TO THE REFORMERS

Yet this prophetic arithmetic was never simple. Some Fathers, like Irenaeus and Lactantius, embraced it eagerly; others, like Origen and Augustine, spiritualized it, transforming the thousand years into symbols rather than countdowns. Medieval chroniclers recalculated the dates; Reformers reignited the hope—and the anxiety. By the modern era, generations of believers had grown up expecting the imminent finale of human history.

This chapter traces that story—from the Jewish apocalyptic roots to the early Church Fathers, from Augustine's sweeping theology, to Reformation literalism—showing how the 6,000-year framework and the Millennium became both a source of hope and a weight upon the Christian mind. It asks how a faith rooted in resurrection and renewal found itself staring at the calendar, convinced that history itself had an expiration date.

MILLENNIALISM AND THE 6,000 YEARS

The idea begins with Scripture itself. A few key biblical passages—read through different lenses across the centuries—sparked both the hope of a coming kingdom and the weight of a cosmic countdown. Chief among them is Revelation 20:1–6, which describes Christ reigning for "a thousand years" after Satan is bound. Yet even from the start, Christians debated whether this "thousand years" was to be understood literally—a real, future kingdom of peace before the final judgment—or figuratively, as a symbol of the entire Christian era between Christ's resurrection and His second coming.

Those who embraced the literal view—often called chiliasm[3] or millenarianism—looked forward to a tangible thousand-year reign on earth. Others, most notably Augustine, argued for a figurative interpretation, seeing the "millennium" as the spiritual reign of Christ throughout history rather than a single future epoch.

The concept of 6,000 years of human history followed by a thousand-year "Sabbath" of divine rest arose from passages like Psalm 90 verse 4 and Second Peter 3 verse 8, which declare that "a day

---

[3] The word chiliasm is derived from the Greek word χίλια (chilia) and its related forms, which mean "a thousand." This noun was formed to mean the doctrine or belief in a thousand-year period. Latin: chiliasmus or chiliastes: The Greek term was adopted into Latin and then passed into English. The initial ch sound in English comes from the Latinized spelling of the Greek letter "chi" (χ).

is as a thousand years with the Lord." Interpreters linked this to the seven days of creation: six "days" (or millennia) of human labor and history, followed by a seventh "day" (the millennium) of divine peace and completion. In this framework, human history itself was mapped onto the very pattern of Genesis.

The roots of this idea ran deep in Jewish thought. Apocalyptic and rabbinic writings before and during the time of Christ often envisioned a messianic age lasting a thousand—or even several thousand—years before the final judgment. Texts like Second Enoch and later rabbinic works, including portions of the Talmud, sometimes spoke of history in terms of "millennial weeks"—six thousand years of struggle and labor followed by a Sabbath Millennium of rest and renewal. Early Christian eschatology inherited heavily from these Jewish traditions, blending the creation-week imagery with messianic expectations.

Early Christian writers carried the theme forward. Irenaeus, in *Against Heresies* (2nd century), explicitly taught the 6,000-year framework, citing both Old and New Testament passages. Lactantius, in the 3rd century, and others echoed the same vision. Yet not all agreed. Origen and, later,

Augustine emphasized the spiritual nature of the kingdom of God, de-emphasizing or even rejecting the literal millennium. By the medieval era, the Church largely followed Augustine's lead, and the 6,000-year scheme faded into the background.

Modern biblical scholarship views the 6,000-year theory as more speculative than authoritative. While Revelation clearly mentions a "thousand years," it never ties this period to the length of world history, nor does Genesis offer such a timetable. The framework instead rests upon a chain of interpretive steps—linking creation days to millennia, reading Psalm 90 and 2nd Peter figuratively, yet numerically; and drawing upon Jewish apocalyptic tradition. Later chronologists, such as Archbishop Ussher with his famous 4004 BC creation date, gave the scheme historical precision it never explicitly claimed for itself.

Today, most scholars see the 6,000-year timeline as a product of theological imagination rather than direct biblical mandate. And the next chapter will reveal that the 6,000-year milestone has already been breached. But for now, the following outline summarizes the development of the literal 6,000-year proposition.

VISUAL EVOLUTION OF THE 6,000-YEAR SCHEME

Biblical Basis

Millennium:

- The primary biblical source is **Revelation 20:1–6**, which speaks of Christ reigning for "a thousand years" after Satan is bound. However, the text itself is **symbolic and apocalyptic** in style, so early Christians debated whether it should be taken **literally** (a real thousand years) or **figuratively** (representing the fullness of God's reign).
    - Literal interpretation → Led to **chiliasm** or **millenarianism**, expecting a real thousand-year kingdom on earth before the final judgment.
    - Figurative interpretation → Augustine and others later saw the "thousand years" as the *entire Christian era* between Christ's resurrection and His second coming.

6,000 years of history:

- This comes indirectly from passages like
  Psalm 90:4 and **2ⁿᵈ Peter 3:8** ("a day is as
  a thousand years with the Lord"),
  combined with the **seven days of creation**
  in Genesis.
  - The idea: Six "days" (6,000 years)
    of human labor/history followed by
    a seventh "day" (1,000 years) of
    divine rest—the Millennium.

Jewish Roots

Jewish apocalyptic and rabbinic traditions **before
and during the time of Christ** included
expectations of a messianic age, often envisioned
as **a thousand, or several thousand years of
peace** before the final judgment.

- Texts like **2ⁿᵈ Enoch** and later rabbinic
  writings (e.g., the *Talmud*) sometimes
  interpret the world's history in "millennial
  weeks"—6,000 years followed by a
  messianic Sabbath.

**Christian millennialism inherits heavily from
Jewish eschatological thought**, especially the
linkage between *creation week* and world history.

27

Early Christian Writings

- *Against Heresies* by **Irenaeus (2nd century)** explicitly taught the 6,000-year framework and the Millennium, citing both Old and New Testament passages.
- **Lactantius (3rd century)** and other early Fathers repeated it.
- But **Origen** and later **Augustine** spiritualized the Millennium, leading the **Medieval Church** to largely drop the literal 6,000-year scheme.

Modern Assessment

- **Biblical scholarship today** generally sees the 6,000-year theory as **more speculative than explicit**.
  - Revelation mentions the "thousand years," but never ties it to world history's length or to Genesis chronologies.
  - The 6,000-year timeline relies on **extra-biblical calculations** (e.g., Ussher's 4004 BC creation date) and **Jewish interpretive traditions** rather than a direct biblical mandate.

28

CHRONOLOGY OF 6,000-YEAR ORIGINS

The **Millennium** comes directly from *Revelation* but is interpreted differently by various Christian traditions. The **6,000-year framework** is **not clearly taught in the Bible itself**; it blends:

- **Jewish eschatology** (messianic age),
- **Creation-week typology**, and
- **Early Christian literalism** (Irenaeus, Lactantius).

Most modern theologians view the 6,000-year world-history scheme as **a theological construct rather than a biblical doctrine**, while the Millennium in Revelation remains a **real biblical image** but open to symbolic interpretation.

Jewish Background (Before Christ)

- **Circa 500–200 BC: Second Temple Judaism**

  - Texts like *1st Enoch* and *2nd Enoch* present cosmic ages and a messianic kingdom.

  - The *Sabbath pattern* emerges: six days of work → one day of rest = six ages of history → final age of peace.

- **Circa 200 BC–AD 70: Apocalyptic Writings**

  o *Book of Jubilees*, *4th Ezra*, *2nd Baruch*: time often divided into symbolic "weeks" or millennia before the Messianic age.

  o The idea that history has **6,000 years** followed by a **1,000-year Sabbath age** circulates in some rabbinic circles.

Early Christianity (1st–3rd Centuries AD)

- **New Testament (circa AD 50–100)**

  o **Revelation 20:1–6** introduces the *"thousand years"* reign of Christ, but gives **no total age of the earth**.

  o **Second Peter 3:8** ("a day is as a thousand years") and **Genesis 1** provide the interpretive seed for 6,000 years plus the Sabbath rest.

- **Apostolic Fathers (circa AD 100–200)**

  - **Epistle of Barnabas (circa AD 100)**: Explicitly teaches six thousand years = six days, followed by a Sabbath Millennium.

  - Strong continuity with Jewish apocalyptic thought.

- **Irenaeus (circa AD 130–202, *Against Heresies*)**

  - Systematizes the 6,000-year doctrine:

    Six days of creation → six ages of history → the seventh day = the millennial reign of Christ.

  - Seen as the earliest *Christian* theological formulation.

- **Lactantius (circa AD 250–325)**

  - *Divine Institutes* repeats the idea: after 6,000 years, the righteous live 1,000 years with Christ before the final judgment.

31

Shifting Interpretation (3rd–5th Centuries AD)

- **Origen (circa AD 185–253)**

    o Allegorical interpreter: the *"thousand years"*; equates to spiritual truths, not literal history.

    o Begins moving away from a concrete 6,000-year timeline.

- **Augustine (354–430)**

    o The book, *City of God* spiritualizes the Millennium as the **entire Christian era** between Christ's first coming and the Last Judgment.

    o His view becomes **dominant in Medieval Western Christianity**.

    o Result: the 6,000-year framework largely fades in mainstream theology.

Medieval to Early Modern Era (500–1700 AD)

- **Medieval Chroniclers** (e.g., Bede, 7th through 8th century)

    o Calculates the earth's age from biblical genealogies (e.g., the *Anno Mundi* system), sometimes noting the 6,000-year idea, but usually without dogmatic force.

- **Ussher Chronology (1650)**

    o Bishop **James Ussher** dates Creation to **4004 BC**, implying the 6,000 years ends around the year **AD 2000**.

    o Fuels later literalists and apocalyptic expectations.

Modern Era (1700–Present)

- **18th and 19th Century Millenarian Movements**

    o Adventists, premillennialists, and other groups revive **literal Millennium** doctrines.

    o Often link 6,000 years to Christ's imminent return.

- **Contemporary Biblical Scholarship**

  o Sees the 6,000-year timeline as **theological tradition, not explicit scripture**.

  o Notes **Jewish apocalyptic origins** and **Christian adaptation,** rather than direct biblical mandate.

CONSEQUENCES FOR CHRISTIAN IMAGINATION

By century's end, generations of believers had been taught to expect the imminent collapse of history.

- **The Shrinking Horizon of Hope**: If the world would soon burn, why invest in curing diseases, exploring space, or stewarding creation? Many Christians embraced an unspoken fatalism: *It's all going to end anyway.*
- **Suspicion of Science and Progress**: Space programs, genetic research, global cooperation—these looked like either distractions or preludes to Antichrist systems.
- **Faith as Fatalism**: The Gospel became associated less with hope for the world than with escape from it.

Inside the Church, it became a standing joke that Revelation's "half-an-hour of silence" was provided for prophecy scholars to adjust their timeline-charts to match how history had actually unfolded. Outside the Church, secular thinkers saw this fatalism and date setting as anti-intellectual, even anti-human. Christianity, in their view, was chained to prophecy charts while the rest of the world reached for the stars.

In the end, the legacy of millennialism and the 6,000-year framework is a paradox. Born from hope for God's kingdom, it too often hardened into anxiety about the world's end. Across centuries, dates were calculated, prophecies charted, and signs scrutinized—yet Christ's return remained beyond human timetables. The Reformers inherited both the expectation and the burden, carrying forward a vision of history always on the brink. As later chapters will explore, this weight of imminence would not stay confined to theology but would begin shaping modern attitudes toward science, progress, and humanity's place in the cosmos.

SEEDS OF RENEWAL

Yet even amid the fever of predictions, some theologians pushed back. They reminded Christians that the kingdom of God was not merely about Futurism.[4] They called for cultural engagement, for stewardship of creation, and for hope that was bigger than any single timetable.

Writers like N. T. Wright emphasized resurrection and renewal rather than escape and destruction. Others argued that prophecy should inspire faithfulness, not fear—courage, not withdrawal.

Slowly, voices began asking whether Christian hope could embrace progress rather than retreat from it, whether believers could anticipate Christ's return without abandoning humanity's call to explore, build, and discover.

---

[4] Futurist eschatology is a Christian interpretation of biblical prophecy, particularly the Book of Revelation, which holds that most of these prophetic texts refer to future events leading up to the second coming of Jesus Christ. Key tenets include the belief in a future Antichrist, a literal Great Tribulation, and in some versions, the Rapture of the Church before these events, with a focus on the literal fulfillment of prophecy, especially concerning Israel and its rebuilt temple.

SETTING THE STAGE

This history explains the burden carried into the twenty-first century: a church looking backward to prophecy while the world looked forward to the stars.

But the question remains: *Must it be this way?*

Is it possible to disentangle Christian hope from the weight of constant imminence? To believe in Christ's return without turning every advance of science, every political event, every astronomical discovery into an apocalyptic omen?

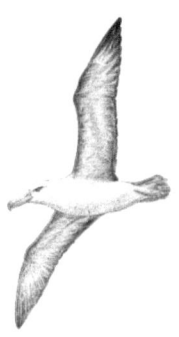

CHAPTER FOUR
THE END OF THE WORLD
AS WE KNOW IT

Isaiah saw it first: a staggering planet, its cities broken, the sky itself peeled back. John, centuries later, wrote of falling stars, fire raining into the seas, and a world gone dark beneath a trembling heaven. At the time, such visions sounded like poetry, or perhaps madness. But we now know what it looks like when a rock from space slams into the earth with apocalyptic power.

We've drilled the crater. We've traced the mega-tsunami. We've modeled the firestorms, the darkness, the poisoned rains. And the language of the prophets, once heard only in pulpits, now echoes in scientific journals.

Geophysical and geochemical studies have mapped the Chicxulub crater at roughly 125 miles wide,[5] confirming seismic energy release equivalent to 100 teratons of TNT[6] Ejecta layers dated to 66 million years ago contain shocked quartz, high iridium concentrations, and tsunami deposits extending across the Gulf region, demonstrating a single catastrophic event of global consequence.

STARS THAT FALL AND SKIES THAT SHAKE

Isaiah 24 speaks of a world convulsed: "The earth staggers like a drunkard; it sways like a hut in the wind; so heavy upon it is the guilt of its rebellion." Elsewhere he sees "the host of heaven dissolved, and the skies rolled up like a scroll."

Jesus repeats the theme: "The stars will fall from heaven, and the powers of the heavens will be shaken."[7] And Revelation adds the most vivid

---

[5] Luis W. Alvarez et al., "Extraterrestrial Cause for the Cretaceous-Tertiary Extinction," *Science* 208, no. 4448 (1980): 1095–1108.

[6] Peter Schulte et al., "The Chicxulub Asteroid Impact and Mass Extinction at the Cretaceous-Paleogene Boundary," *Science* 327, no. 5970 (2010).

[7] Matthew 24:29 (ESV/NIV etc.) — "Immediately after the tribulation of those days the sun will be darkened, and the

images of all: "The stars of the sky fell to the earth, as the fig tree sheds its winter fruit when shaken by a gale... something like a great mountain, burning with fire, was thrown into the sea... a great star, blazing like a torch, fell on a third of the rivers."[8]

In the ancient world, physical "stars" simply meant bright things in the sky—meteors, comets, fireballs. And we have seen them fall. The Leonid meteor storm of 1833 filled the sky with so many streaks of fire that whole towns thought the end had come. Yet those were only pebbles. The Bible's imagery points to something far larger.

When the Sky Really Does Fall

On the morning of February 15, 2013, a roughly 65-foot diameter asteroid exploded over Chelyabinsk, Russia, with roughly 30 times the energy of the Hiroshima bomb. It shattered windows across 200

---

moon will not give its light; and the stars will fall from heaven, and the powers of the heavens will be shaken."

[8] Revelation passages including Revelation 6:13; Revelation 8:8-11, etc. (e.g., *"stars... fell to earth as a fig tree sheds its winter fruit when shaken by a gale"; "a great star blazing like a torch..."*) — these are vivid apocalyptic images of celestial disturbance.

square miles, injuring around 1,600 people.[9] In 1908, a much larger object flattened about 770 square miles of Siberian forest at Tunguska.

But even these pale beside the giant that ended the Age of Reptiles.

As scientists have dated the event, sixty-six million years ago, a 6 to 9-mile diameter asteroid struck the edge of what is now the Gulf of Mexico at Chicxulub. The impact created a cavity nearly 124 miles wide and 12 to 19 miles deep—piercing the earth's crust. A wall of seawater taller than skyscrapers raced outward. Rock vapor and molten debris shot high into the stratosphere, then fell back through the atmosphere like a global rain of fire. Forests burned. Soot and sulfur gases wrapped the planet in darkness. Photosynthesis stopped. Food chains collapsed. Roughly 75% of Earth's species vanished, including the non-avian dinosaurs.[10]

---

[9] Chelyabinsk airburst (2013): ~20 m asteroid, large atmospheric explosion, damage over a wide area from windows, injuries, etc. (Historical/modern astronomical/planetary defense records).

[10] Chicxulub impact event (~66 million years ago): The asteroid's diameter estimated ~10-15 km; kinetic energy massive. Creation of a crater ~180-200 km in diameter, tens

What Isaiah called a drunken, reeling earth is exactly what the planet would feel like under seismic waves from an impact releasing millions of times the energy of the largest human bomb ever built.

The Younger Dryas Puzzle

Scientists have even argued that a smaller impact, about 12,900 years ago, may have triggered the Younger Dryas —a rapid return to near-glacial cold, just as the longer, historic Ice Age seemed to be ending. Proponents cite platinum spikes in Greenland ice cores,[11] Nano-diamond rich layers,[12] and charcoal horizons across North America as evidence of widespread wildfires. Critics argue for

---

of kilometers deep in places. Global tsunami waves, massive ejecta, stratospheric dust, global firestorms, darkened skies, ecosystem collapse. Studies modeling the global tsunami in *AGU Advances* (2022) confirm devastating flooding of nearly all coastlines worldwide, geological evidence in over 100 sites supporting wave paths and effects.

[11] Nicholas Petaev et al., "Large Pt Anomaly in the Greenland Ice Core Points to a Cataclysm at the Onset of Younger Dryas," *Proceedings of the National Academy of Sciences* 110, no. 32 (2013): 12917–12920.

[12] James P. Kennett et al., "Nanodiamonds in the Younger Dryas Boundary Sediment Layer," *Science* 323, no. 5910 (2009): 94–94.

volcanic or meltwater explanations,[13] noting chronological inconsistencies in radiocarbon sequences. The consensus remains unsettled, with impact hypotheses gaining, but not securing, majority acceptance.

But if correct, it shows that even in humanity's early memory, the sky may have struck hard enough to change history.

ECHOES OF REVELATION

Now re-read Revelation:

- *"A great mountain, burning with fire, was thrown into the sea, and a third of the ships were destroyed."* An ocean impact would launch a tsunami across entire basins. The Chicxulub wave left enormous ripples, or "mega-ripples," roughly 52 feet high in what is now Louisiana; Revelation imagines whole navies swept away.[14]

---

[13] Vance T. Holliday et al., "Comprehensive Analysis of the Younger Dryas Impact Hypothesis," *Quaternary Science Reviews* 247 (2020): 106489.

[14] Megatsunami evidence: The Chicxulub impact tsunami was modeled globally; shoreline inundation, flow velocities, seafloor scouring, and "megaripples" in what is now Louisiana (~16 m average wave height in some deposits)

- *"The sun became black as sackcloth... the moon like blood."* Firestorms and stratospheric dust after Chicxulub dimmed the sun for years!
- *"A great star, blazing like a torch, fell on the rivers... and many people died from the bitter waters."* Impact plumes can seed the atmosphere with nitric and sulfuric acids, turning rains acidic and freshwaters foul.[15]

The parallels do not prove John *saw* an asteroid. Yet, they do show how closely apocalyptic language mirrors the actual physics of a cosmic strike.

NO WARNINGS, NO COUNTDOWN

Jesus insisted that, *"no one knows the day or the hour."* Impacts arrive the same way. The Chelyabinsk asteroid came from the sunward sky—undetected until it was already here. Even

---

match model predictions of wave height and sediment disturbance.

[15] Acidic rains / bitter waters analogues: While Revelation uses "Wormwood" to describe water turned bitter (Rev. 8:10-11), scientific studies of large impacts show that vaporization of target rocks and atmospheric injection of sulfur and nitrogen compounds can lead to acid rain and poisoning of freshwaters. (Models of impact winter / geochemical studies associated with mass extinction boundaries.)

today, with telescopes and satellites, we have found only a fraction of the "city-killer" objects that cross Earth's orbit.

When the next big one comes, there will be no calendar of omens, only the sudden voice of the Creator who rules the sky as well as the soil.

The Lamb's Book of Life

And here the prophets pivot. The falling stars, the roaring seas, the staggering earth,—all of it matters less than this: *"If anyone's name was not found written in the book of life, he was thrown into the lake of fire."* Revelation assures that for those whose names are written in the Lamb's book—the same moment of cosmic terror, becomes the doorway to resurrection. Paul writes, *"The dead in Christ will rise first… then we who are alive, who are left, will be caught up… to meet the Lord in the air."* The judgment is real, the end of the world as we know it is certain, but so is the promise of life beyond it.

A Closing Image

Isaiah saw the earth lurch and the sky roll back. John saw fire fall and waters roar. Science now gives us names—asteroid, bolide, impact winter—

for the things the prophets only described. But neither telescope nor seismograph can change the point of their visions:

The end will be sudden. The Judge will be just. And those who belong to the Lamb will rise when He calls, even if the very crust of the earth has split beneath their feet!

When Scripture speaks of "the end," it rarely indulges in the drips-and-drabs of a slow-motion finale. The prophetic cadence is sudden, global, unmissable; "the day of the Lord" arriving not with a calendar of milestones to check off, but like a thief who chooses the one hour no one expects. Isaiah hears the planet itself convulse; Jesus warns of ordinary life rolling on right up to that moment; Peter declares the heavens themselves will roar and dissolve. The portrait is not of a countdown we can manage, but of a consummation God commands.

THE EARTH'S LAST CONVULSION

Isaiah 24 gives perhaps the starkest Old Testament canvas for a terminal judgment: the earth "emptied," its surface "twisted," its structures shaken down, its inhabitants scattered without distinction. It is the end of complacent normalcy and of human hierarchies alike: "as with the people, so with the priest... buyer... lender... creditor." Isaiah's language escalates from social leveling to geophysical collapse: "the earth is broken... split... violently shaken... reels like a drunkard"—until the whole order falls and "does not rise again." The emphasis is unmistakably planetary, not provincial.

If modern readers hear in this a dim resonance with extinction events or global phase-changes, Isaiah's purpose is higher and holier: judgment for covenant-breaking rebellion, and the clearing of the stage for the Lord's universal reign. The text does not supply a timeline of precursors; it supplies a verdict. When the Judge stands, the earth gives way.

JESUS ON THE END: SUDDEN, PUBLIC, INESCAPABLE

In Matthew 24 Jesus intertwines immediate, first-century trauma (the fall of Jerusalem) with the cosmic consummation, but when He speaks of His appearing, the pattern is clarity itself: it is public ("as lightning"), definitive, and—critically—unexpected. He undercuts date-setting with a single sentence: "Concerning that day and hour no one knows... but the Father only." Then He gives the feel of the world on the brink: not apocalyptic "countdown cosplay," but weddings and meals and payrolls and fieldwork. As in Noah's day, ordinary life hums along "until" the moment arrives. Normalcy is not proof of safety; it is the context of surprise.

This unexpectedness is not incidental; it is theological. To live under the Father's unknown hour is to live in readiness rather than in rumor. Across the New Testament, the repeated simile for the Second Coming[16] is the "thief"—not because the coming is secret, but because it is unforeseeable. The moral: stay awake; do not presume a warning shot.

Peter's Cosmology of the Day

Peter takes up the same refrain. "The day of the Lord will come like a thief," he writes; the heavens pass away "with a roar," the "heavenly bodies" (or "elements") are "burned up and dissolved," and the earth's works are exposed. The scope is cosmic; the tempo is sudden. Peter's pastoral point lands in ethics, not esoterica: if this is the horizon, live holy and hopeful now. The

---

[16] Gr. *parousia*: the presence of one coming, hence, the coming, arrival, advent.—Thayer's Greek Lexicon, electronic database by Biblesoft, Inc.

emphasis again falls away from a parade of preliminary signs and onto the surprise of the event and the quality of our watchfulness.

No Ongoing Signs Required

Taken together, Isaiah 24, Matthew 24, and 2nd Peter 3 do not teach a necessary sequence of ongoing signs that the Church must tick off before Christ can return; they teach that the event will arrive decisively, universally, and unexpectedly. Jesus forbids day-and-hour calculation; He depicts society proceeding with ordinary cares "until" the moment. Peter echoes the thief-in-the-night motif to stress suddenness, not a visible pre-timeline. This does not deny that tribulations occur in history; it denies that we can infer God's clock from them. The appropriate response is alert faithfulness—not prophetic arbitrage.

The Voice That Raises the Dead

What, then, actually happens to God's people at the end? Jesus Himself gives the simplest answer: "An hour is coming when *all who are in the tombs* will hear his voice and come out." There is no narrower gate here than the voice of the Son—no esoteric knowledge, no survivalist strategy, no earthly ark to board—only the call of Christ that pierces cemeteries. Those who belong to Him rise "to the resurrection of life."

Paul supplies the pastoral complement: the Lord descends "with a cry of command, with the voice of an archangel, and with the trumpet of God," and "the dead in Christ will rise first," joined by the living saints to meet Him. The note is assurance for the anxious, not ammunition for speculation: "Therefore encourage one another with these words."

NAMES KEPT—AND KEPT FROM FEAR

The hope that steadies believers under an unknown hour is not decoding headlines but being known by the Lamb. Scripture names this assurance the "book of life," opened at the final examination when the dead stand before God. To put the importance of the security of the soul into perspective, consider Jesus' response after the Disciples returned from a mission of miracles: "Nevertheless do not rejoice in this, that the spirits are subject to you, but rather rejoice because your names are written in heaven."[17] Those enrolled belong to the Lamb and enter His city; their vindication does not rest on successfully reading the times, but on being written in His book. This is why the Church can live awake without living afraid.

A Note on "Ages" and Endings

It is historically coherent to speak of the "Age of Modern Man" arising after the last Ice Age and to note that civilizations rise and fall amid smaller and larger ecological shocks. Scripture does not dispute such observations; it simply announces an ending that no geology could schedule: an unveiling in which the Judge returns, the world-order is shaken to its foundations, and creation passes through fire to renewal. The Bible's "end" is the end *as we know it*—the termination of death's dominion, the exposure of every work, and the public enthronement of the King. It is not the end of God's purpose, but the end of our presumption.

---

[17] Luke 10:20.

GENEALOGIES AND ARCHAEOLOGICAL DATING

The Masoretic Text (MT)

The Masoretic Text forms the bedrock of nearly all modern Old Testament translations, preserved by generations of Jewish scribes between the sixth and tenth centuries AD. Descending from much earlier Hebrew manuscripts, the **Masoretes** standardized not only the consonantal text but also introduced vowel-pointing and meticulous marginal notes to guard its transmission. Their work, carried out in centers such as Tiberias and Babylon, reflected a near-reverent precision: every letter counted, every line tallied, every column checked for accuracy before a manuscript was deemed fit for use in synagogue or scholarship. The result was a Hebrew Bible stabilized in form and sound—a text shaped by Jewish tradition and received by both Judaism and, eventually, Protestant Christianity as the authoritative Old Testament witness.

The Septuagint (LXX)

Centuries before the Masoretes, however, another tradition emerged along the sunlit shores of Hellenistic Egypt. Around the third century BC, Jewish scholars in Alexandria translated the Hebrew Scriptures into Greek, producing what came to be known as the Septuagint—or simply the "LXX," named after the legend of **seventy translators** laboring in harmony. Intended for Greek-speaking Jews scattered across the Mediterranean, the Septuagint became the Bible of the Early Church; New Testament writers quoted it freely, and Christian theologians from Irenaeus to Augustine read Israel's story through its account. Yet the LXX sometimes diverges from the later Masoretic tradition in wording, chronology, and even content—with differences especially noticeable in the primeval genealogies of Genesis chapters 5 and 11. These textual streams, Hebrew and Greek, would carry parallel versions of sacred history into the Christian era, setting the stage for debates over which numbers—and which narrative—best preserve the ancient past.

MASORETIC TEXT VS. SEPTUAGINT

In the Masoretic Text, the begetting ages in Genesis 5 and 11 are generally lower; in the Septuagint, they are typically 100 years higher for most patriarchs. That single pattern pushes the Septuagint's creation date 1,400 to 1,500 years earlier than the MT-based Ussher (4004 BC). Nineteenth-century author, William Hales argued on text-critical grounds that

54

the longer Septuagint figures are often original and preferred, yielding a date of creation circa 5411 BC rather than 4004 BC. According to Hales' chronological findings, modern Septuagint reconstructions commonly land in the mid-5500s BC (e.g., around 5554 BC), which is about 1,386 to 1,500 years longer from Adam to Abraham than deduced from the Masoretic Text.

Hales' New Analysis of Chronology (1830)[18] systematically compared Masoretic Text and Septuagint genealogies, concluding that the Septuagint's begetting ages restore an older textual tradition, aligning Genesis 5 and 11 with Second Temple chronology. Modern recalculations (e.g., Bickerman, 1988[19]; Tov, 2012[20]) broadly affirm the textual independence of Septuagint figures, though debates persist on whether scribal harmonization or theological motives drove these divergences.

---

[18] William Hales, *A New Analysis of Chronology and Geography, History and Prophecy*, vol. 1 (London: C.J.G. & F. Rivington, 1830).

[19] Elias Bickerman, *Chronology of the Ancient World* (Ithaca, NY: Cornell University Press, 1988).

[20] Emanuel Tov, *Textual Criticism of the Hebrew Bible* (Minneapolis: Fortress Press, 2012).

THE BEGINNING OF THE
AGE OF MODERN MAN

If one reads Genesis genealogies as stylized (telescoped) lines rather than exhaustive father-to-son registers, the Septuagint's already "longer" clock becomes a floor rather than a ceiling. This lets biblical chronology sit more comfortably beside what archaeology shows about post-Ice-Age lifeways: complex ritual sites, proto-urban towers, and the forerunners of farming within a few millennia after the Younger Dryas. In other words, using the LXX (instead of the MT), plus a realistic view of genealogical compression, shifts the "beginning" of the Age of Modern Man to a horizon that coheres with early Holocene developments rather than forcing everything inside a compressed 6,000-year scheme.[21]

A FEW EMBLEMATIC FINDS

Archaeology now catalogs thousands of radiocarbon determinations across Epi-Paleolithic and early Neolithic sites in the Levant and Anatolia.

---

[21] On the magnitude of the LXX extension vis-à-vis the Masoretic Text, see Smith's synthesis.

These radiocarbon determinations are dense enough to map cultural change through the Younger Dryas into the Holocene. High-precision AMS dating at Göbekli Tepe,[22] Jericho,[23] and Abu Hureyra[24] consistently places monumental architecture, proto-urban planning, and early cultivation within the range of 9600 to 8000 BCE. These datasets collectively anchor the rise of complex societies immediately post–Younger Dryas, well before the compressed 6,000-year biblical horizon derived from MT chronologies.

Illustrative examples:

(1) **Göbekli Tepe**—monumental, megalithic ritual enclosures built by hunter-gatherers in the **Pre-Pottery Neolithic** between roughly **9600 and 8200 BC**, i.e., just after the last Ice Age ended.[25]

---

[22] Dietrich et al., 2013.

[23] Kathleen Kenyon, *Excavations at Jericho* (London: British School of Archaeology in Jerusalem, 1981).

[24] Andrew M. T. Moore et al., "Village on the Euphrates: From Foraging to Farming at Abu Hureyra," *Proceedings of the Prehistoric Society* 66 (2000): 1–40.

[25] Klaus Schmidt and Jens Notroff, "Göbekli Tepe: A Stone Age Sanctuary in South-Eastern Anatolia," *Documenta Praehistorica* 40 (2013): 239–256.

(2) **Jericho's Neolithic wall and tower**—massive stone architecture from **PPNA circa 8300 to 8000 BC**, signaling communal planning and proto-urban organization.

(3) **Abu Hureyra (Syria)**—a classic sequence documenting the shift from foraging to cultivation around the Younger Dryas/Holocene transition, with AMS dates confirming continuous occupation and early cereal cultivation. These aren't outliers; they are headline cases within a broad, well-dated landscape of early Holocene sites that collectively move the onset of recognizably "modern" human-social complexity to the very end of the last Ice Age.

WHY THE 6,000-YEAR SCHEME IS ALREADY OVERSHOT

Hales' system alone, which dates creation at **5411 BC**, would result in a present age of the earth of 7,400 years from creation to **AD 2025**. By Hales estimate, the current Age is already 1,400 years beyond the hypothetical 6,000-year window.

Contemporary LXX-advocating chronologists (e.g., S. Douglas Woodward)[26] likewise argue that the biblical timeline should add about **1,500 years,** compared to the MT/Ussher reckoning; Woodward explicitly urges switching from KJV/MT to the LXX because it "adds over **1,500 years** to the biblical timeline in Genesis 1–11," and he often frames creation at around **7,500 years** ago rather than 6,000. In short: based on either Hales' classic LXX-leaning chronology or Woodward's modern defense of the same observations, "the Age of Man" has already exceeded the 6,000-year theory by about fifteen centuries—before we even consider genealogical telescoping or the archaeological record's much deeper horizons.

HOW TO LIVE BEFORE THE SIREN

Because the end is certain and its timing concealed, the ethic for God's people is simple:

- **Stay awake, not alarmed.** Readiness is moral, not manic; Jesus warns against sleep, not about calendars. "Therefore, stay awake… you also must be ready."

---

[26] S. Douglas Woodward, *Rebooting the Bible: Part 2*, Faith Happens 2020.

- **Hold loosely to the present order.**
  Isaiah's vision disenchants us from the
  illusion of permanence; Peter's dissolving
  elements unhook us from the idolatry of
  what can burn. Holiness and hope, not
  hoarding, are the appropriate strategy.
- **Fix on the voice.** The same Christ, who
  calls sinners now, will call sleepers then.
  Our preparation is to belong to Him today;
  trusting that the next voice we hear at the
  world's last convulsion will be the One
  that raises us!

When the end arrives, it will not be the triumph of
chaos, but the triumph of a Person. The earth may
stagger; the heavens may roar; ordinary plans may
be interrupted mid-sentence; but the Son will
speak, the dead will answer, and the names He
keeps will stand. No more clocks to wind, no more
omens to collect—only the Lamb, the book He
authored with His blood, and the creation remade
to fit His glory. Live now for that voice; and the
end of the world as we know it, will be the
beginning of life as He promised.

The next chapter will explore this possibility—a way of framing Christian hope that lifts the albatross from humanity's shoulders, freeing faith to inspire rather than hinder forward motion into the cosmos.

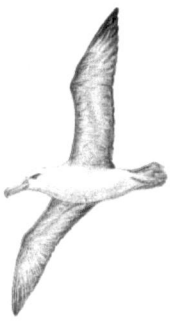

CHAPTER FIVE
RAISING THE OUTLOOK

*Toward a faith large enough for both prophecy
and progress.*

The twenty-first century stands at a threshold of
wonders. We split atoms, map genomes, peer into
galaxies fourteen billion light-years away, and
dream of boots on Mars and beyond. Artificial
intelligence learns languages; private companies
plan moon colonies; telescopes capture the faint
afterglow of the Big Bang itself.

And yet, for millions of Christians, the horizon of
hope remains strangely narrow. Sermons still warn
that history teeters on the brink of closure.
Bestsellers continue to speculate about Antichrist
governments, Middle Eastern wars, and the next
prophetic "sign." For many, the world's story feels
already finished—its timeline expired. The result is
a faith trapped between two worlds: looking
anxiously for Christ's return while standing amid
the greatest age of discovery since the Renaissance.
And the burden grows heavier with each scientific
advance, as though progress itself defies prophecy,

as though every rocket launched into space stretches the tension between heaven's timetable and humanity's aspirations.

This chapter asks a simple question: *Must Christian-hope always carry this weight?*

REDISCOVERING THE KINGDOM'S HORIZON

The Christian imagination has too often shrunk prophecy to a countdown-clock. For many modern believers, Christ's return functions like the final page of a book already read. Yet Scripture presents the kingdom of God in richer colors:

- It is **already here**: Jesus declared the kingdom "at hand," breaking into history through his life, death, and resurrection.
- It is **not yet complete**: Paul spoke of creation groaning toward renewal, of Christ reigning until every enemy is defeated, including death itself.
- It is **cosmic in scope**: Revelation ends not with souls escaping the earth but with heaven descending, uniting the realms of God and creation in a renewed cosmos.

This vision reframes history not as a collapsing tent but as a story moving toward consummation. Christ's return is not merely the *end* of history; it is the *fulfillment* of history. That fulfillment may come tomorrow—or in ten thousand years. Scripture leaves the timeline **deliberately open**, calling every generation to faithfulness without demanding anxiety about dates and signs.

PARABLES OF THE LONG DELAY

If Christian history has often felt burdened by a sense of ticking imminence, the words of Christ Himself tell a more nuanced story. His own parables repeatedly point to an **extended and indeterminate interval** between His departure and His return—a gap designed to shape the Church's character more than its calendars. Again and again, Jesus frames the Kingdom not as an event crashing into the present moment, but as a reality advancing through time with servants laboring faithfully while the Master is away.

This theme emerges clearly in parables that speak of **far countries**, **long journeys**, **delayed arrivals**, and **masters who return after a long time**. Far from teaching an immediate apocalypse, these stories invite disciples to live faithfully across the open-ended centuries of God's providence, a vision broad enough to encompass not only the last two millennia but, if necessary, tens of thousands of years into the future.

PARABLES EXPLICITLY MENTIONING DELAY

The first example comes in **Luke 19:11–27**, the *Parable of the Minas*. Luke sets the scene with a critical note: Jesus had given this parable specifically: "because they supposed that the kingdom of God was to appear **immediately**." His story subverts that very expectation. A **nobleman goes into a far country** to receive a kingdom and only *then* returns, placing resources in the hands of servants and leaving them to labor faithfully during his absence. The entire narrative hangs on this extended departure; the nobleman's return is certain, but the time in between is neither short nor predictable.

Similarly, the *Parable of the Talents* in **Matthew 25:14–30** presents the Kingdom as "a man **going on a journey**" who entrusts his property to servants. Matthew adds a striking phrase: "**After a long time** the master of those servants came and settled accounts with them." The point is unmistakable—the delay is long and deliberate, designed to test stewardship, not to satisfy curiosity about dates.

The *Parable of the Ten Virgins* in **Matthew 25:1–13** makes the same point through the image of a **bridegroom who is delayed**. As the delay stretches on, the wise virgins keep their lamps ready while the foolish ones run out of oil, illustrating that faithfulness requires preparation for the *long haul*, not just excitement for the first hour.

In **Matthew 24:45–51**, the *Faithful and Unfaithful Servant* story shows the unfaithful servant saying to himself, "My master **is delayed**." Instead of watching and working, he exploits the postponement for selfish gain—only to be caught unprepared when the master finally returns.

Jesus drives the point home again in **Mark 13:34–37**, describing the Son of Man as "a man **going on a journey**, when he leaves home and puts his servants in charge." The command to "keep awake" has nothing to do with setting dates and everything to do with long-term readiness amid uncertainty. Even the *Parable of the Wicked Tenants* in **Mark 12:1–12** uses this same motif: a vineyard owner "**went into a far country**," sending servants over a long interval before finally sending his son. The emphasis once again points to the owner's extended absence; beginning with the time it would take to travel to a distant location and highlighting the tenants' faithful stewardship.

Finally, **Luke 12:35–40** pictures servants waiting for their master to return from a wedding feast, keeping their lamps burning through the night until his unannounced arrival. The servants' posture of **watchfulness during delay** fits perfectly with the broader theme: the Master's return is certain but not scheduled.

THE THEOLOGICAL WEIGHT OF THE DELAY

What do these parables accomplish?

First, they correct **premature expectations**. Luke tells us directly that Jesus spoke the *Minas Parable* because His listeners imagined the Kingdom arriving immediately. Instead, He gives them a story of distance, stewardship, and waiting—a theological horizon stretched far beyond their immediate moment.

Second, they build a framework for **open-ended time**. Phrases like "after a long time" and "the master is delayed" refuse to quantify the interval. The deliberate vagueness leaves room for decades, centuries, even millennia without contradiction. The focus falls on *faithfulness amid waiting*, not on speculation about calendars.

Third, the apostles later reinforce this vision. Peter writes, "With the Lord one day is as a thousand years, and a thousand years as one day. The Lord is **not slow** to fulfill His promise... but is **patient** toward you."[27] God's timetable transcends human impatience. Jesus' parables and Peter's theology sing in harmony: divine delay serves divine purposes.

The **Unknown Hour** Principle frames the entire discussion. Jesus insists that, "no one knows the day or hour," a statement meant not to frustrate but to free believers from obsessive prediction making. The parables illustrate this freedom: servants live well, steward faithfully, build wisely, and watch expectantly—not because they know the date, but because they do not.

IMMINENCE AS POSTURE, NOT PREDICTION

Some object that the New Testament often speaks of Christ's coming as "near" or "soon." But read in context, this language summons vigilance, not chronology. The Church is to live **as if** Christ could come at any time, while working **as if** He may not come for many millennia yet.

---

[27] 2nd Peter 3:8–9.

Jesus' parables embody this tension perfectly. They call for **active readiness** rather than **passive countdowns**. They invite faithfulness in farming, building, exploring, learning, and laboring—not apocalyptic panic at every eclipse or earthquake. The Master's delay is long by design. It shapes discipleship into *patient faithfulness*, not frantic date setting.

Perhaps, more than in any of His parables, Jesus alluded to the need for the perseverance of the saints by asking this brief, but haunting question: "When the Son of Man comes, will he find faith on the earth?"[28] This question truly evokes considering that it might be many more thousands, or even tens-of-thousands of years until Earth's final cataclysm and Christ's simultaneous return.

The oldest New Testament manuscripts record Jesus as saying, "concerning that day and hour no one knows, not even the angels of heaven, nor the Son, but the Father only."[29] This statement obliterates the notion that any human could possibly know the time of the Second Coming.

---

[28] Luke 18:8.

[29] Matthew 24:36 (ESV).

And, taken together, Christ's words demand the possibility that His return might be so far into the future that Christian faith would no longer be found on the earth.

IMPLICATIONS FOR CHRISTIAN HOPE

If Jesus Himself foresaw a long and indeterminate interval then the weight of constant imminence, so often felt throughout Christian history is obviously self-imposed, rather than divinely required. His parables envision centuries—or millennia—of human history unfolding under God's providence, affording time: to discover, to build, to explore, to steward the earth and perhaps even the stars.

Far from denying His return, this long view dignifies the present. It allows believers to anticipate Christ's coming **without abandoning humanity's vocation** to cultivate, to create, and to seek understanding of God's world. The Master will return—but until then, the lamps must stay lit, the vineyards tended, the talents invested. Faithfulness flourishes in the midst of this tension between the certainty of Christ's return, and the uncertainty of the timing.

CHRIST'S KINGDOM AS RENEWAL

What would it mean for Christians to believe in Christ's return without fearing humanity's forward motion?

It would mean rejecting the false choice between **prophecy and progress**, between awaiting Christ and embracing the future. Exploration would no longer feel like rebellion against divine sovereignty. Scientific discovery would no longer seem like a rival to biblical faith.

The Church has often forgotten that *curiosity itself*—the drive to seek, to know, to create—is part of bearing God's image. From Adam naming the animals to modern scientists mapping the cosmos, human exploration reflects divine intention, not opposition.

To fear progress is to distrust the very gifts of intellect, creativity, and stewardship that have been entrusted to humanity. As Dorothy Sayers once wrote, "The creative will of man is God's will in him." Faith should bless this creativity, not burden it with suspicion.

TOWARD A THEOLOGY OF
COSMIC RESTORATION

The problem lies not in biblical prophecy itself but in its popular distortion. The New Testament never instructs believers to calculate dates or treat history like a secret code. Instead, prophecy functions as an *invitation* to live faithfully in light of God's ultimate purposes.

- It comforts the suffering: assuring them that injustice and death will not have the final word.
- It warns the complacent: reminding them that history belongs to God, not empires.
- It inspires courage: calling believers to endure, create, serve, and hope until Christ returns—whenever that may be.

Seen this way, prophecy expands the Christian imagination rather than shrinking it. It offers ultimate meaning without demanding immediate timelines. It blesses human endeavor rather than burdening it with dread.

A THEOLOGY FOR THE SPACE AGE

If the twentieth century baptized prophecy into apocalyptic urgency, the twenty-first century needs a theology big enough for the stars.

Such a theology would affirm:

1. **The cultural mandate still stands** – Humanity's call to "fill the earth and subdue it" (Genesis 1:28) includes cultivating knowledge, beauty, justice, and discovery.
2. **Christ's return will not waste history** – Every act of creativity, stewardship, and exploration contributes to the unfolding story God is writing through humanity.
3. **Faith can bless progress** – The same God who governs history also delights in human courage to build, learn, and dream beneath the galaxies he made.

Imagine a Christianity that inspires astronauts, scientists, and engineers rather than standing apart from them—a faith confident that no discovery will surprise God, no frontier will threaten his reign, no human achievement will hasten or delay Christ's return.

The notion aligns with the mandate of Genesis 1:28 as interpreted in modern theological works,[30] which frame human exploration, technological innovation, and environmental stewardship as extensions of divine vocation rather than secular rebellion.[31] Recent space ethics scholarship[32] likewise calls for integrating moral theology into debates on planetary colonization and AI governance.

LIFTING THE ALBATROSS OF APOCALYPTIC FEAR

To lift this albatross is to set faith free from the burden of immediacy. It is to say: Christ will return—but until he does, let us build, explore, and discover with courage, hope, and reverence. Such a faith would no longer treat prophecy as a chain restraining human progress but as a horizon expanding it.

---

[30] N. T. Wright, *Surprised by Hope: Rethinking Heaven, the Resurrection, and the Mission of the Church* (New York: HarperOne, 2008).

[31] J. Richard Middleton, *A New Heaven and a New Earth: Reclaiming Biblical Eschatology* (Grand Rapids, MI: Baker Academic, 2014).

[32] Charles S. Cockell, *The Meaning of Liberty Beyond Earth* (Cham: Springer, 2021).

It would no longer demand retreat from the world but joyful engagement with it. It would no longer pit Heaven against Natural History. Then the man beneath the two skies could lift his eyes without fear—seeing prophecy, not as a weight upon his shoulders but as wind in his sails, carrying him forward into both faith and discovery without contradiction.

LOOKING AHEAD

The next chapter will explore practical implications of this vision. How might churches, schools, and Christian thinkers embrace a theology of exploration? How can Christians recover a sense of cosmic wonder without losing the hope of Christ's return? For if faith is to speak meaningfully in the age of space travel and artificial intelligence, it must offer more than escape from history. It must offer hope for its fullness.

CHAPTER SIX
FAITH BENEATH
EXPANDING SKIES

***Building a Christianity unafraid of science,
discovery, and the future.***

Theologians write of God's transcendence, how the heavens cannot contain Him, how the universe itself rests in His hand. Yet in practice, many modern Christians speak as though God were threatened by human curiosity, as though telescopes and rockets could trespass on divine territory.

The time has come to recover a faith as vast as the cosmos itself—a faith able to bless astronauts and astronomers, geneticists and geologists, dreamers and discoverers. A faith that expects Christ's return but does not dread human achievement in the meantime.

This chapter asks: *What would it look like for Christianity to breathe deeply beneath expanding skies?*

RECLAIMING WONDER AS WORSHIP

The first step is to see scientific discovery not as a rival to faith but as a form of wonder. Scripture is full of references to awe of God's creation:

- "The heavens declare the glory of God" (Psalm 19:1).
- God speaks to Job out of the whirlwind, describing storehouses of snow, constellations bound by cosmic cords, wild creatures beyond man's understanding (Job chapters 38 through 41).
- Paul declares that God's "eternal power and divine nature" are "clearly seen" in the things He has made (Romans 1:20).

To explore creation, then, is to step into worship—not to threaten it. Telescopes peering into distant galaxies, microscopes uncovering the machinery of cells, satellites mapping cosmic radiation—none of these devices shrink God. They expand human awe before Him.

When Christians recover this sense of wonder, faith no longer feels opposed to discovery. Science becomes a doxology, not a danger.

TEACHING A LARGER HOPE

The second step is theological: teaching believers to distinguish between *imminence* and *urgency*. These two contextual views may simply be stated as:

- **Imminence**: Christ may return at any time.
- **Urgency**: Therefore, the world has no future worth building.

The first is biblical; the second is not.

Jesus' parables often describe servants faithfully at work when the master returns—not passively waiting for history to collapse. The apostles planted churches, wrote letters, trained leaders, and urged believers to live holy and productive lives—all under the conviction that Christ could come at any moment.

A mature Christian eschatology should therefore encourage:

- **Cultural engagement** rather than retreat.
- **Long-term vision** alongside short-term faithfulness.
- **Hopeful investment** in human flourishing rather than fatalistic resignation.

Churches and schools can teach prophecy as *promise* rather than *prediction*—a source of courage instead of a lifeless display of charts.

WELCOMING SCIENTIFIC CURIOSITY

Many scientists dismiss Christianity because they perceive it as hostile to progress. Yet the problem often lies not in Scripture itself but in its popular interpretation. When believers suspect that every scientific breakthrough threatens biblical faith, they create a false choice: God or genetics, Christ or cosmology, faith or physics. But Scripture never demands this opposition. Imagine if Christians became the loudest voices; blessing:

- Space exploration as an extension of humanity's God-given stewardship.
- Medical research as obedience to Christ's call to heal and serve.
- Environmental science as care for God's creation rather than idolatry of it.

Such a posture would surprise skeptics and invite dialogue rather than hostility. It would show that Christian hope expands to meet every new horizon rather than retreating before it.

ANSWERING THE CAUTIOUS BELIEVER

Some Christians fear that embracing science and exploration might dilute faith or ignore prophecy. But a larger vision does not dismiss Christ's return; it simply refuses to weaponize it against human flourishing.

Below are some common misapprehensions, and suggestions on how these might be resolved.

- **Objection:** "If the world will end, why invest in it?"
  - o **Response:** Because Christ commanded stewardship until He comes.[33] Faithfulness means cultivating creation, not abandoning it.
- **Objection:** "Won't science lead people away from God?"
  - o **Response:** Science reveals *how* creation works; faith asks *why it exists at all*. The two questions need not compete.

---

[33] Luke 19:13.

- **Objection:** "Isn't space exploration prideful—like building Babel?"
  - o **Response:** Babel sought to replace God; exploration seeks to understand His universe. Humility, not hubris, should guide discovery.

A thoughtful theology can therefore welcome progress without idolizing it, honor prophecy without fearing the future, and love Christ's return without fleeing the present.

PRACTICAL STEPS FOR CHURCHES AND THINKERS

1. **Preach a Theology of Vocation**
   - o Show that engineers, scientists, artists, and teachers all share in God's creative work.
2. **Incorporate Science into Christian Education**
   - o Host lectures, astronomy nights, or museum trips that celebrate both faith and scientific knowledge.
3. **Support Christian Voices in Science**
   - o Highlight astronauts, researchers, and medical professionals who see their work as worship.

4. **Encourage Long-Term Vision**
   o Teach students to imagine careers, discoveries, and contributions that may bless generations beyond their own lifetime.

5. **Pray for Human Flourishing**
   o Include prayers for scientists, policymakers, and explorers as often as for missionaries and pastors.

Such steps form a Christianity confident enough to bless the future.

FAITH AS THE WIND, NOT THE WEIGHT

When faith recovers this larger vision, the albatross begins to lift.

No longer chained to apocalyptic timetables, Christianity can speak with hope rather than dread. No longer suspicious of science, it can bless human curiosity as a gift rather than a threat. No longer trapped beneath competing skies of prophecy and progress, it can stand beneath both—seeing Christ as the Lord of history and the Lord of the cosmos alike.

ALBATROSS — C.W. Steinle

The man beneath the two skies may finally straighten his shoulders. Faith will no longer hang like a dead weight across his neck but carry him forward into the vast story of God's universe—until Christ Himself brings that story to its fullness.

CHAPTER SEVEN
FAITH FOR A NEW FRONTIER

***How Christianity could shape culture, ethics, and
exploration in an age of discovery.***

Humanity has always carried its beliefs into new
worlds. Medieval sailors stitched crosses onto the sails
of their caravels. Renaissance artists painted biblical
scenes on the domes of new cathedrals. Early scientists
like Kepler and Newton described their work as
uncovering God's artisanship in creation's design.

But the modern age has often portrayed faith as a
relic of the past—something to be left behind on
Earth while humanity journeys outward into the
stars. Part of this comes from faith's own retreat:
decades of apocalyptic anxiety have made
Christianity appear suspicious of science, allergic
to progress, and indifferent to the future.

But what if the opposite were true? What if
Christian faith freed from the albatross of
immediacy could help guide humanity through the
moral, artistic, and spiritual challenges of a rapidly
changing world?

This chapter explores what such a faith might look like—and how it could shape the emerging frontier.

ETHICS AMONG THE STARS

Every new technology brings ethical dilemmas: nuclear power, genetic engineering, artificial intelligence, planetary colonization. Science can tell us what *can* be done; it rarely asks whether it *should* be done. Christianity, at its best, has always answered the questions of meaning, morality, and human dignity. A forward-looking faith could:

- **Ground ethics in the image of God:** affirming that human life has worth not because of utility or intelligence but because of divine creation.
- **Guide decisions about artificial intelligence:** ensuring machines serve human flourishing rather than enslaving or replacing it.
- **Shape environmental stewardship:** urging colonization efforts on Mars or the Moon to consider whether any ecological missteps might have been avoided here on Earth.
- **Set limits on technology's pride:** reminding humanity that power without wisdom leads to Babel, not blessing.

Rather than surrendering ethics to secular voices alone, Christians could speak with courage and compassion into debates about AI, climate, medicine, and space exploration—bringing moral clarity.

THE ARTS OF A LARGER HOPE

Science opens the frontier; art gives it meaning.

Imagine music inspired not by dread of the end but by awe before the galaxies. Picture films and literature exploring the drama of human courage and divine mystery across cosmic landscapes. Envision paintings and sculptures capturing not only the God of history, but the God of the nebulae, the quasars, the black holes—as they bend light itself. For too long, Christian art has tended to focus inward—concerned only with private devotion or narrow moral lessons. A faith as large as the cosmos could inspire the artistic media of:

- **Music**—blending worship with wonder at creation's vastness.
- **Literature**—exploring faith amid alien worlds, deep time, and human ambition.
- **Architecture**—that draws the eye upward, reflecting galaxies and starlight in sacred spaces.

Where imagination expands, faith follows. Beauty opens doors that arguments alone cannot.

SCIENCE, FAITH, AND THE PUBLIC SQUARE

Public discourse often pits "science" and "religion" as opposites. Yet many of history's greatest scientists—Kepler, Pascal, Faraday, Mendel—were people of faith who saw no contradiction between the telescope and the Bible. A Christianity free from the weight of imminent apocalypse could:

- **Partner with science** in education, funding, and exploration, rather than disregarding these critical areas of influence.
- **Support research** in medicine, energy, and technology as expressions of responsible stewardship.
- **Shape public policy** with moral wisdom rather than fueling conspiracies and apocalyptic fears.

Such engagement would surprise both skeptics and believers accustomed to hostility between the Church and the laboratory. It would show that faith thrives not by retreating from modernity but by guiding it toward justice, beauty, and sustainability.

TOWARD A THEOLOGY OF EXPLORATION

Colonizing the Moon, mining asteroids, terraforming Mars—these are not merely engineering challenges. They raise profound spiritual questions:

- What does it mean to bear God's image on another planet?
- How do we carry justice, mercy, and humility into spacefaring civilizations?
- If we should indeed meet other intelligences, what does the Gospel mean for them?

Christianity, when unafraid of such questions, can offer a theology big enough for the universe. It can see exploration not as escaping Earth but as extending stewardship, creativity, and curiosity into every corner of God's cosmos.

ANSWERING THE CRITICS

Some skeptics will insist that religion should stay out of science and politics altogether. Others will claim Christianity has only ever opposed progress. Yet history tells a more complex story:

- Monasteries preserved learning throughout the European Dark Ages.
- Cathedrals became centers of art, music, and architecture.
- Universities like Oxford and Harvard began as Christian institutions.
- Modern science itself emerged in cultures specifically shaped by the belief in a rational Creator.

The problem was never faith itself but the moments when faith shrank—when fear eclipsed wonder, when timetables replaced hope, when prophecy became paralysis. A renewed Christianity could admit its past mistakes while recovering its older, richer role as the patron of learning, art, and exploration.

FAITH WITHOUT THE ALBATROSS OF FATALISM

When faith sheds the burden of immediacy, it can breathe again. It can speak to the twenty-first century not as a relic of the past but as a companion for the future.

- To scientists, it can offer humility in the midst of mystery

- To politicians, it can offer ethics shaped by human dignity.
- To artists, it can offer beauty rooted in divine transcendence.
- To explorers, it can offer courage to trek the boundless skies.

Such a faith does not retreat from the modern world; it guides it. It does not fear the next frontier; it blesses it. It does not demand the end of history; it embraces the fullness of history.

And perhaps that is how the man beneath the two skies will finally walk forward—beneath prophecy and progress, faith and discovery, heaven and earth—without the albatross across his shoulders.

CHAPTER EIGHT
THE CENTURY AHEAD

Envisioning a faith unafraid of the future.

The twenty-first century opens like a dawn over uncharted seas. Rockets rise from launch pads like prayers of fire. Telescopes peer beyond galaxies into the first faint light of creation. Artificial intelligence translates languages, guides surgeons, composes music, and writes poetry. Medicine vanquishes diseases once thought immortal. Engineers dream of cities on Mars, green energy across deserts, and water drawn from barren air.

And yet, amid such wonder, humanity carries questions of meaning, morality, and mortality as old as Eden. For what good are rockets if men carry war into the stars? What use are colonies on Mars if injustice and hatred follow us there? What value is intelligence—artificial or human—if it lacks wisdom, humility, and hope?

This century will demand more than technology. It will demand vision. And if Christianity lifts the weight of imminence and learns to bless the future rather than fearing it, it could help craft a civilization that is worthy of its discoveries.

A FUTURE FOR SCIENCE AND FAITH TOGETHER

Imagine a world where universities no longer pit science against faith but see them as partners in seeking truth. Theology classrooms teach the wonder of quantum physics alongside the mystery of divine transcendence. Physics labs host lectures on ethics shaped by centuries of Christian moral thought.

Churches sponsor observatories, science fairs, and space scholarships, seeing telescopes as tools of worship rather than threats to belief. Scientists and theologians meet not to debate boundaries but to explore meaning—together pondering the vastness of a universe still expanding at the speed of light.

Such a future would surprise those who assume faith must always oppose progress. It would show that Christianity freed from apocalyptic suspicion could bless the scientific imagination rather than discouraging it.

SPACEFARING STEWARDSHIP

Picture the first permanent settlement on Mars, not merely as a human achievement but as a spiritual milestone. Chapels rise beside laboratories. Hymns mingle with the hum of oxygen generators. Ethical debates about terraforming, AI governance, and planetary mining unfold with voices shaped by Christian visions of stewardship and justice.

Colonists read Genesis not as an excuse to exploit worlds but as a call to care for them: *Fill the earth and subdue it* becomes *tend and keep,* a charge to cultivate rather than conquer. The same faith once accused of retreating from progress now provides the moral compass for humanity's first steps beyond Earth.

THE ARTS OF A COSMIC IMAGINATION

In this envisioned century, art blossoms beside science. Composers write symphonies inspired by images from the James Webb Space Telescope. Filmmakers create epics about faith and courage amid alien landscapes. Painters fill cathedrals with cosmic vistas, showing Christ not only as the Lord of Earth, but also as the Lord of the physical heavens—of galaxies and gravitational waves.

Such art lifts the human spirit beyond materialism, reminding explorers and scientists alike that life requires beauty as much as oxygen, meaning as much as mathematics.

ETHICS FOR AN AGE OF POWER

Technology will tempt humanity toward hubris: genetic engineering, artificial intelligence, planetary control. But Christianity at its best has always spoken of humility, justice, and the limits of power.

In this future, Christian ethicists help guide laws on AI rights, genetic editing, and planetary colonization. Pastors preach sermons on humility before creation. Theologians write books on the image of God amid machine learning and alien ecosystems.

Faith embellishes technology with wisdom.

WORSHIP BENEATH ALIEN SKIES

One day, perhaps centuries from now, a congregation will gather on another world. Dust storms may swirl outside domes of steel and glass. Yet inside, voices will rise in hymns not of fear but of wonder—thanking God for the stars, for the Christ who reigns over galaxies, for a Gospel wide enough to embrace a universe billions of light-years across.

Such worship will carry no hint of the albatross, no fear that exploration delays Christ's return, no suspicion that discovery threatens divine sovereignty. Faith will stand confident, joyful, unafraid—its hope as vast as the heavens themselves.

THE END WITHOUT THE ENDING

Christ may return tomorrow, or in ten thousand years. Faith need not know the timing to live faithfully. A Christianity free from apocalyptic anxiety will embrace this mystery, working for justice, beauty, knowledge, and hope as though history may last a thousand millennia—while living with the readiness that it may end tonight.

This paradox—urgency without panic, hope without fear—will define the faith of the future.

WALKING FORWARD BENEATH TWO SKIES

The man beneath the two skies will finally straighten his shoulders. The prophecy-sky above him will no longer thunder with doom, but shine with promise. The science-sky will no longer compete with faith, but expand it.

No longer racing against time, humanity will walk forward into history's next chapters with courage, humility, and hope.

And perhaps the true marvel of the century ahead will not be colonies on Mars or artificial intelligence or telescopes glimpsing the universe's edge.

Perhaps it will be this:

that faith and discovery learned at last to walk together beneath the stars.

PART II

THE ALBATROSS OF GODLESS EVOLUTION

CHAPTER NINE
BENEATH TWO SKIES AGAIN

The man stood beneath two skies...

One sky stretched cold and ancient across the night, its galaxies measured not in miles but in time itself. Every point of light was a courier from ages past—ten thousand years, a million years, a billion years—its journey across the void a silent rebuke to the notion of a young, enclosed world.

Astronomers spoke of redshifts and cosmic background radiation, of a universe expanding from a single moment of origin toward ends unfathomed. Its very silence whispered of creation as a process, of stars forging heavy elements in their cores, of planets coalescing from cosmic dust across epochs so long the human mind can scarcely imagine them.

But the other sky was not silent:

It spoke in syllables of flame: *"Let there be light."* It told of a Word through whom all things were made, of a Creator whose Spirit hovered over the waters before there was earth or sun or moon to mark a day. It told of a Christ who entered history and walked out of death itself; the Resurrection a defiance of every closed system the first sky seemed to impose. This sky was charged with purpose, with miracles, with promises as old as Adam—and as new as the empty tomb.

And the man, standing beneath both heavens, felt the weight of their opposition; or what seemed like opposition. For the first sky with its fossils and galaxies and DNA-strands left little room for miracles, for souls, for the Incarnation of God in flesh. And the second sky, to the modern mind, appeared too narrow for the first: too small for a cosmos fourteen billion years deep. He wondered if these two skies, like rival monarchs, had divided the empire of human thought between them: Science claiming the realm of facts, Faith entrenched in the realm of meaning. Matter on one throne; Spirit on the other. And between them the human mind, stretched seemingly to the breaking point.

But perhaps the skies were not rivals after all.

THE WEIGHT OF TWO VISIONS

For the modern believer, the burden grows heavier with every scientific discovery. The specter of Darwin hovers over biology, geological ages stretch the earth's history far beyond Archbishop Ussher's 4004 BC, and telescopes peer so deeply into space that they gaze back toward the birth of time itself. The speed of light—186,000 miles per second—functions as both messenger and historian, carrying to our eyes the glow of galaxies millions of light-years away, so distant their light began its journey before the first human spoke the first word.[34]

Materialism—our age's "natural"[35] philosophy—takes this data as proof of a godless cosmos.

---

[34] The speed of light is about 670 million miles per hour meaning that a light-year is roughly equal to the distance of 5.88 trillion miles.

[35] In 1 Corinthians 2:14-16, Paul draws a sharp contrast between what he calls the natural man (Greek: *psuchikos*, or sometimes translated "soulish," "unspiritual," "worldly") and the spiritual man (Greek: *pneumatikos*). He writes:

"The natural person does not accept the things of the Spirit of God, for they are foolishness to him, and he is not able to understand them because they are spiritually discerned."

The natural man, according to Paul, lives in the realm of what can be observed, experienced by the senses, or reasoned out

The universe, it says, is a closed system of matter and energy, governed by impersonal laws, producing life and consciousness through blind processes alone. Evolution, in this telling, needs no divine mind, no guiding purpose; it sculpts through mutation and selection, through chance and necessity, and it tells its story across billions of years without ever lifting its eyes toward heaven.

Here lies the albatross: the weight of a worldview that declares spirit, miracle, and even meaning itself to be illusions—useful, perhaps, for human comfort, but with no more ultimate reality than dreams.

MATERIALISM AND THE QUESTION OF MIRACLES

The Christian story rises or falls on miracles. Creation itself is presented not as accident but command: *"And God said... and it was so."* The Resurrection of Christ stands as the central miracle of history, a divine act breaking the rule of death itself.

---

apart from spiritual revelation. Because the spiritual truths depend on the Spirit of God, the natural person cannot grasp them—they seem irrational or merely symbolic. Meanwhile, the spiritual man "appraises all things," i.e. is able to evaluate spiritual realities because of the Spirit.

Philosophers like David Hume scoffed, claiming uniform human experience testifies against miracles. Nature, he argued, does not break her own laws. Yet the Christian reply was never that miracles violate nature's order, but that they reveal nature to be open to its Author—that the One who wrote the laws may also at times, write in the margins.

A purely material cosmos leaves no such margins. It confines reality to what can be weighed and measured, rendering consciousness itself a kind of cosmic accident, the human longing for transcendence a mere biochemical quirk. Against this, the Christian insists that the Resurrection was not metaphor but event—that history itself turned on a supernatural hinge when Christ stepped out of the tomb. If that miracle stands, then the universe is not a closed box of atoms and void, but a theater for both natural law and divine freedom.

WHAT IS A DAY?

Much of the modern conflict between faith and science turns on a single word in Genesis: ***Day***. Was creation accomplished in six literal, twenty-four-hour periods? Or does the text's first chapter speak in the language of poetry and symbol, its "days" unfolding across epochs whose length only God knows?

Early interpreters like Augustine warned against reckless literalism, noting that the sun itself—the very marker of an earthly day—does not appear until the fourth "day" of creation; meaning this "first mention" of the word cannot be defined by the motions of an earth and sun which have yet to be created. The Hebrew word *yōm* can indeed mean a twenty-four-hour day, but also an indefinite span: "the day of the Lord," "the day of trouble," "in the day you eat of it."

Modern science, for its part, testifies to a universe billions of years old. Geology measures ages in strata and isotopes; astronomy measures time in starlight. Physics traces cosmic history back to the first fractions of a second after the Big Bang. Light from distant galaxies began its journey long before human history—before, even, the earth itself had cooled from its primordial fires.

Some, like the physicist Gerald Schroeder, have tried to bridge the gap with relativity itself: time, they note, dilates under cosmic expansion so that six "days" from one frame of reference might equal billions of years in another. Others adopt the "day-age" view, reading Genesis as a theological hymn rather than a geological manual. The "gap theory" inserts vast ages between Genesis 1:1 and 1:2; still others speak of an "ancient earth" whose history long predates Adam.

Yet beneath all these debates lies a deeper question: Must faith and science war over the length of a day, or can both serve the same truth, each in its own tongue?

CONSCIOUSNESS AND THE HUMAN SOUL

Materialism struggles to explain not only miracles but also minds. Why should atoms, arranged by blind forces, awaken to beauty, morality, and meaning? Why should a universe indifferent to love produce creatures who write symphonies, who grieve their dead, who ponder eternity?

Christianity answers: because the human soul bears the image of its Maker. We are not merely clever animals; we are creatures in whom earth and heaven meet—matter and spirit woven together by the breath of God.

If consciousness, morality, and reason point beyond neurons and chemistry, then the materialist's account proves too small for the data of human experience. The heavens may declare the glory of God. But so does the human mind that contemplates them!

TOWARD DIALOGUE BETWEEN FAITH AND SCIENCE

The man beneath the two skies feels the weight of their apparent opposition: evolution against creation, materialism against miracle, science against faith.

Yet perhaps the opposition is false.

Perhaps the God who called light out of darkness also authored the long processes by which galaxies spin and genes recombine. Perhaps the same Word through whom all things were made entered His creation not to deny its history but to redeem its future.

For the truest burden is not scientific discovery, nor even the vastness of time and space, but the notion that faith must fear these things—that the God of Genesis cannot also be the Lord of quarks and quasars, of fossils and photons, of every deep history written in the rocks and the stars.

If Christ indeed rose from the dead, then no age of the earth, no depth of space, no theory of biology can finally exclude the hand—or the heart—of God!

In the chapters to come, we will follow this widening horizon: through the debates over Darwin and Genesis, through the philosophies of time and creation, through the testimonies of miracles and the mysteries of consciousness, toward a vision of faith unafraid of science and science unchained from materialism—a faith as vast as the skies under which the man still stands, looking upward.

CHAPTER TEN
THE MIRAGE OF
MATERIALISM

The man stood beneath the stars and heard a whisper from the modern age:

"Matter is all there is."

It was the creed of laboratories and lecture halls, of textbooks and telescopes, a doctrine seldom spoken aloud yet assumed everywhere: the universe is a closed machine, its gears grinding from the Big Bang to the Heat Death[36] of all things with no hand upon the controls. Matter and energy, plus time and chance, are the whole story. There is no Author. There is no Voice saying *"Let there be light."*

---

[36] The heat death of the universe, or Big Freeze, is a hypothetical scenario where the universe reaches maximum entropy, leading to a uniform temperature and a state where no thermodynamic free energy remains to sustain motion or life. In this state, all stars would have burned out, black holes evaporated, and the universe would become a cold, dark, and diffuse expanse of subatomic particles.

There is no eternal Word through whom all things were made.

This vision has a certain grandeur. It paints galaxies across the blackness, traces the long climb of life from single cells to symphonies. It tells of apes who became men and men who became scientists, peering ever deeper into the clockwork of the cosmos. It promises knowledge without superstition, progress without providence, a universe free of angels and demons and divine decrees.

But it also leaves the soul hollow. For, if materialism is true then the story of the cosmos has no chapters, no plot, no goal. It does not *mean* anything. It merely *is*. The stars burn; the atoms collide; the genes replicate; the species evolve; the minds that arose from chemistry contemplate their own extinction; and the universe, vast and silent rolls on, indifferent.

THE WEIGHT OF A CLOSED UNIVERSE

Materialism wears the mask of certainty. It claims the authority of science, the rigor of reason, the mantle of inevitability. It tells us that all phenomena—life, thought, love, morality—must eventually be reduced to physics and chemistry, for nothing exists outside them.

This worldview says, the miracle is not that Christ rose from the dead, but that anyone believes such a thing in the age of microscopes and particle accelerators. Matter is all; spirit is illusion; the supernatural is a leftover superstition from the age of ignorance.

Yet this confidence conceals a deep fragility. For materialism, when pressed, cannot explain itself.

It cannot explain why a universe of blind forces should produce minds capable of *knowing* those forces. It cannot account for moral obligation in a cosmos indifferent to good and evil. It cannot tell us why beauty moves us, why love binds us, why truth matters. If thoughts are only the buzzing of neurons shaped by natural selection for survival rather than for truth, then even the belief in materialism dissolves into a by-product of chemistry, no more valid than a dream or a fever.

As C.S. Lewis once observed, to see through everything is the same as not to see at all. A philosophy that explains away mind, meaning, and morality ends by explaining away itself.

THE EXILE OF TRANSCENDENCE

Still, materialism seduces with its promise of control. It offers mastery over nature, technologies that heal, build, and connect; rockets that pierce the heavens that were once thought divine. It teaches us to ask not *"Why?"* but *"How?"*—not "Who made the stars?" but "What are they made of?" And in doing so, it slowly exiles transcendence from the human imagination.

The ancient world looked up and saw the heavens declaring the glory of God. The modern world looks up and sees nuclear fusion. The ancients heard thunder and thought of divine voices; we hear only atmospheric electricity. The rainbow was once a sign to Noah; now it is only refraction in droplets of water.

Nothing wrong with that, says materialism. The world is what it is: atoms, void, and nothing more.

But in stripping the world of divine presence, materialism also strips it of ultimate meaning. We gain the mechanics of the rainbow and lose its covenant. We chart the chemical basis of love and lose its poetry. We explain the firing of neurons in the brain and lose the mystery of consciousness itself.

SCIENCE WITHOUT SCIENTISM

Here we must distinguish science from scientism.

Science is a method, a disciplined way of studying the natural world. It has given us antibiotics and space telescopes, quantum theory and genetic sequencing. It does not claim omniscience; it advances by questions, by experiments, by the humility to revise its own theories in the face of new evidence.

Scientism, by contrast, is a philosophy masquerading as science. It insists that only what can be measured is real, that anything beyond the reach of experiment—God, soul, morality, even consciousness itself—must be illusion or irrelevance.

But this is not a scientific claim; it is a metaphysical one. And it collapses under its own weight, for the statement *"only what can be measured is real"* cannot itself be measured. It is not physics; it is dogma.

True science need not wear these shackles. Many of history's greatest scientists saw their work as confirming the rationality of God. The laws of nature, they believed, were not enemies of faith but expressions of divine order. Modern materialism forgets this heritage.

115

THE MIRAGE EXPOSED

Materialism promises liberation from superstition, but it delivers instead a world without wonder. It offers knowledge but cannot account for knowledge; it offers life but drains it of meaning; it explains the rainbow's colors but not its beauty, the brain's chemistry but not the mind's thoughts, the survival of genes but not the drama of good and evil, love and loss, hope and despair.

It tells us that the Resurrection cannot happen because closed systems do not open. It tells us that creation by divine word is myth because physics needs no Author. Materialism tells us that miracles are impossible because they do not fit inside its box—even as the box itself rests on assumptions it cannot justify.

And yet the human heart rebels. It senses that consciousness is more than neurons, that morality is more than instincts, that love is more than biochemistry, that beauty is more than survival strategy. It suspects, in other words, that the materialist's universe is too small for the reality we actually inhabit.

TOWARD A WIDER HORIZON

If the universe is not a closed machine but a creation, then its laws are not the whole story. They are the grammar, but not the Author. The mechanism, but not the meaning.

The Christian claim is not that science is false, but that reality is larger than science alone can measure. The heavens declare the glory of God: through hydrogen and helium, through galaxies and gravity, through equations and experiments— but glory nonetheless.

Materialism offers a mirage: a world that seems to explain everything except itself, a cosmos full of facts but empty of meaning. To lift this albatross from modern thought, we must recover a vision in which science and faith are not enemies but partners in wonder, each pointing beyond the mirage to the reality that grounds both reason and revelation.

In the next chapter, we will turn to miracles—not as violations of nature, but as signs that nature itself is open to the One who called it into being, the One in whom, as Scripture says, *all things hold together*.

CHAPTER ELEVEN
THE QUESTION OF MIRACLES

The man beneath the two skies wondered what it would take for heaven to break in.

For the modern world whispers that heaven never has, that heaven never will—that the cosmos rolls on like a sealed machine, indifferent to prayers, deaf to prophets, empty of divine interruptions. Science, we are told, has closed the door on miracle. Nature is a locked house, and its keys belong to mathematics alone.

But if the house is locked, who locked it? And is it locked at all?

THE SKEPTIC'S CHALLENGE

No name looms larger over the modern dismissal of miracles than the previously mentioned David Hume. In the eighteenth century, the Scottish philosopher argued with elegant severity that no testimony could ever be sufficient to prove a miracle.

Why? Because, Hume claimed, our uniform experience tells us that nature's laws do not break. The sun rises; the dead stay dead; water does not turn to wine; people do not walk on waves or rise from graves. If someone reports such an event, the sensible conclusion is that the witness is mistaken or deceived, not that nature's laws have been suspended.

Hume sharpened his point, asking: Which is more likely? that the whole framework of natural law collapsed for one brief moment, or that fallible human beings made an error? The answer, he said, is obvious.

So for centuries, philosophers and skeptics echoed Hume's verdict: miracles are irrational, unscientific, and unworthy of belief.

THE CHRISTIAN REPLY

But the Christian reply was never to deny the regularity of nature. It was to deny Hume's cramped definition of reality.

For Hume assumed that the universe is a closed system, that nature itself is ultimate, that whatever lies beyond it—if anything does—can never act within it. But Christianity insists that nature is not ultimate; God is. The laws of physics describe the ordinary patterns of creation, but the Author of those patterns is free to write new sentences whenever He wills.

Thomas Aquinas, centuries before Hume, had already defined miracles, not as violations of nature but as events whose cause transcends nature. When Christ turned water into wine, He did not break chemistry; He simply exercised a power beyond it. When He rose from the dead, He did not abolish biology; He acted as the Lord of life itself.

In other words, miracles are not chaos invading order. They are higher order breaking into lower order—the Composer playing a new melody on an instrument He Himself designed.

THE RESURRECTION AS THE CRUX

All this leads to the miracle at the heart of Christianity, the Resurrection of Jesus.

The apostle Paul wrote with startling frankness: *"If Christ has not been raised, our preaching is useless and so is your faith."*[37] Christianity stakes

---

[37] 1st Corinthians 15:14.

everything on this event. It is not a metaphor for springtime renewal or psychological courage; it is the claim that death itself has been broken, that history turned a corner when a crucified man walked out of His own tomb.

The historical case has been made in every generation:

- The empty tomb, acknowledged even by early opponents.
- Eyewitness testimony of hundreds, recorded within decades.
- The birth of a movement willing to die for its belief in a risen Lord.
- The failure of alternative explanations—hallucinations, conspiracies, legends—to account for the explosive growth of the earliest Christian witness.

If the Resurrection happened, then reality is open to divine action, and Hume's argument collapses. For the question is no longer, whether nature's laws are uniform, but whether the Author of nature has acted in history so that history itself bears His fingerprints.

MIRACLES BEYOND THE BIBLE

Nor does the witness to divine action end in the first century.

Across ages and cultures, reports of miracles persist: healings beyond medical explanation, near-death experiences defying neuroscience, visions and conversions; and providences that refuse to fit inside the materialist box. Skeptics dismiss them all; believers debate the skeptics; philosophers puzzle over them. Yet the sheer recurrence of such testimonies suggests that human experience stubbornly resists confinement to mere mechanism.

C.S. Lewis noted that miracles cluster around moments of revelation—Moses before the burning bush, Elijah on Mount Carmel, Jesus at Cana and Calvary. They are not magic tricks; they are signs, pointing beyond themselves to the purposes of God.

And so the question is not whether miracles break the laws of nature, but whether nature itself is part of a larger story—one in which the Author may at times, write in bold letters across the page.

THE OPEN UNIVERSE

Materialism pictures the cosmos as a machine. Christianity pictures it as a creation.

A machine grinds on, indifferent to meaning. A creation lives by the will of its Creator, sustained in being from moment to moment. Its laws are real, its regularities reliable—but it is never sealed against the interventions of its Maker.

The Incarnation itself—the Word made flesh—is the ultimate declaration that heaven and earth are not separate realms but overlapping realities. If God can dwell among us in Christ, then the gap between natural and supernatural is not absolute. The house of creation is not locked; its door stands open to the One who built it.

MIRACLES AND MEANING

Ultimately, the debate over miracles is a debate over the kind of universe we inhabit.

If the cosmos is closed, then miracles are impossible by definition, whatever the evidence. If the cosmos is open to its Creator, then miracles are not intrusions but revelations—moments when the veil lifts and the deeper logic of reality flashes forth.

The Resurrection, then, is not a violation of nature but the beginning of a new creation, the first fruits of a world in which death itself, will one day be undone.

The next chapter will turn to time itself—its length, its mysteries, its relation to creation. For beneath the two skies lies not only the question of whether God acts, but when, and on what scale of days and ages His purposes unfold.

CHAPTER TWELVE
TIME AND CREATION

The man beneath the two skies looked up and wondered not only *what* the heavens declared, but *when* they had begun to speak.

For time itself seemed to stretch without edge or anchor. The stars above told stories in light-years, their glow beginning its journey across space long before the first human stood on the earth to see it. The rocks beneath his feet spoke in ages—strata laid down in fire and flood, fossils pressed between layers older than imagination. The physicists told of cosmic background radiation, an echo from the birth of the universe itself, nearly fourteen billion years ago.

THE FIRST EVENINGS, THE FIRST MORNINGS

The opening chapter of Genesis is a symphony of creation: light and darkness, sea and sky, land and life, sun and moon, stars and seasons, all rising at the word of God.

Its refrain, *"and there was evening, and there was morning,"* beats like a drum between each act. For the Creator, to speak is to accomplish; His word is deed, His command reality. Yet, the "days" of Genesis may not measure hours but order, not chronology but liturgy—the pacing of a cosmic temple being built for the glory of God.

Many have read the "days of creation" as literal days, defending a young earth only thousands of years old. For them, geology is explained by a single catastrophe, fossils by flood, the speed of light itself perhaps altered to fit the timeline. The world, they insist, is not older than Adam by more than a few rotations of the earth.

But the universe itself seems to argue otherwise.

THE TESTIMONY OF THE COSMOS

Astronomy stretches human imagination to the breaking point. Light travels nearly six trillion miles in a single year, yet we see galaxies whose light began its journey millions—even billions—of years ago. Geology speaks of ages before ages: continents drifting, mountains rising, oceans carving valleys through stone laid down in forgotten epochs.

As the man looked up at the stars, he realized he was watching a ballet on a galactic scale. As the universe has expanded over the last 13.8 billion years, the regions of space that emitted the light we now see have moved farther away. This means that objects whose light left 13.8 billion years ago are now much more distant. A calculation based on the standard cosmological model (known as Lambda-CDM) shows that these objects are now at a "comoving distance" of about 46.5 billion light-years from Earth. The calculation is based on data collected by major space-based and ground-based observatories and is constantly being refined.

- Planck Satellite (ESA): The Planck mission, which operated from 2009 to 2013, provided the most precise all-sky map of the Cosmic Microwave Background (CMB) to date. The data released by the Planck team in 2013 and 2015 refined the age of the universe and the values of the cosmological parameters used to calculate its size.[38]

---

[38] Planck Collaboration, N. Aghanim et al., *"Doppler boosting of the CMB: Eppur si muove," Astronomy & Astrophysics* 571, A27 (2014), arXiv:1303.5087.

- Wilkinson Microwave Anisotropy Probe (W-M-A-P): Before Planck, NASA's W-MAP mission produced detailed full-sky maps of the cosmic microwave background's temperature variations.

- Hubble and James Webb Space Telescopes: These telescopes use multiple methods to measure distances and redshifts of galaxies, which inform our understanding of cosmic expansion.

The universe's "ballet" of movement is observed using geometrical calculations considering various parallax angles of view.[39] This advanced form of "triangulation" shows the precise speed and direction of every heavenly body. Gravity supplies the inward pull; motion supplies the outward inertia; and the result is a cosmos where

---

[39] Parallax is the apparent shift in an object's position due to a change in the observer's position, and the parallax angle is half the total angular shift observed over a baseline. A larger parallax angle indicates a closer object, while a smaller angle signifies a more distant one. This principle is used to measure distances to astronomical objects, with the unit of distance known as a parsec defined by a parallax angle of one arcsecond over a baseline of one astronomical unit (the distance from Earth to the Sun).

orbits persist for eons because moving masses follow curved paths under gravity's pull (inertia vs. gravity in balance).

Earth itself was made to move: it spins, it circles the Sun, the Sun sweeps around the Milky Way, and our whole neighborhood drifts through the cosmos relative to the primordial afterglow of creation— the cosmic microwave background. At the equator, Earth's spin is about 1,037 miles per hour.[40]

COSMIC MICROWAVE BACKGROUND

From the moment scientists discovered it in 1965, the **Cosmic Microwave Background** has been regarded as one of the most important clues to the origin and structure of the universe. It is sometimes called the "afterglow" of the Big Bang, the faint whisper of radiation that fills all of space like the dying embers of a once-roaring fire. Roughly 380,000 years after the Big Bang, when the young cosmos had expanded and cooled enough for electrons and protons to combine into neutral atoms, the fog of scattering particles cleared. For the first time, photons—the particle units of light—

---

[40] Space.com, "How fast is Earth moving?," equatorial rotation ≈1,037 mph.

could travel freely across space. The radiation released at that moment has been racing outward ever since; stretched by cosmic expansion until today, it shines not in visible light but in microwaves at a temperature of 2.73 Kelvin (that is, minus 454.8 degrees Fahrenheit), just a few degrees above absolute zero.

To modern cosmology, this thin bath of microwaves is much more than an exotic curiosity. It is a cosmic landmark, a remnant from the earliest era of physical creation, and one of the most precise tools available for studying both the history and motion of the universe itself. When satellites like **C-O-B-E**, **W-MAP**, and **Planck** mapped the sky in exquisite detail, they found the CMB to be astonishingly uniform, the same in every direction to one part in 100,000. Yet there was a subtle pattern: a tiny rise in temperature on one side of the sky and a tiny dip on the other.

This "dipole anisotropy," as it came to be called, could be explained very simply.[41] If you are at rest with respect to the expanding universe, the CMB

---

[41] Particle Data Group, *"Cosmic Microwave Background,"* in *Review of Particle Physics* (2024), section "Cosmic Background Dipole Measurements," p. 29.

should look the same in every direction—no side hotter or colder than any other. But if you are moving relative to that cosmic frame, the photons ahead of you get compressed by your motion, their wavelengths shortened, making them appear slightly hotter. Those behind you, by contrast, are stretched and cooled. The result is a faint hot-cold pattern across the sky, a kind of cosmic Doppler shift that directly reveals your speed relative to the universe itself.[42]

Careful measurements show that our Solar System is moving at about 825,000 miles per hour relative to this universal rest frame defined by the CMB. The direction of this motion points roughly toward the constellation Leo, reflecting not only Earth's orbit around the Sun but the Sun's own orbit around the center of the Milky Way; plus, the Milky Way's motion toward the Andromeda galaxy, and the entire Local Group of galaxies moving through the larger cosmic web. Layer by layer, when astronomers correct for these known motions, what remains is the

---

[42] M. Piat et al., "Cosmic background dipole measurements with the Planck," *Astronomy & Astrophysics* 571, A26 (2014).

net velocity of our whole galactic neighborhood through the expanding universe itself.

The CMB frame has thus become the closest thing modern cosmology has to a "preferred frame of reference"—not in the sense of overturning Einstein's relativity, for the laws of physics remain the same everywhere—but as a practical benchmark tied to the universe's own birth. It anchors our measurements of large-scale structure, galaxy flows, and cosmic expansion, providing a backdrop against which the drama of cosmic motion unfolds.

One might picture it this way: imagine a vast swimming pool filled with millions of ping-pong balls bobbing on the surface. In the frame of the pool itself, the balls drift randomly, no side favored over any other. But if you begin swimming through the pool, balls in front of you come thicker and faster; those behind thin out. The CMB behaves in just this way, its nearly uniform glow betraying our motion through space not by any single point of light, but by a universal, all-encompassing shift in temperature from one horizon to the other.

As instruments grew ever more sensitive—from the early C-O-B-E maps in the 1990s to W-MAP in the 2000s and finally Planck's stunning full-sky survey in 2013—the precision of these measurements improved dramatically. Modern results even account for the way our motion subtly aberrates the small-scale fluctuations themselves, a cross-check confirming the reality of the speed we measure. Far from being a mere curiosity, the dipole in the CMB has become one of the most solidly established facts in cosmology, a reminder that our Earth, Sun, and galaxy are all carried along in the vast river of cosmic expansion.

For those wanting to explore further, excellent introductions can be found in the Planck Collaboration's 2013 paper, *"Doppler boosting of the CMB"*[43]: the standard *Planck 2018 results* published in *Astronomy & Astrophysics*, and countless summaries in modern cosmology textbooks and reviews. Together, they show how a faint whisper from the dawn of time became a measuring stick for the motion of galaxies themselves—and for our own small place in the moving, restless universe.

---

[43] *Eppur si muove* (arXiv:1303.5087).

How Fast is Earth Moving?

The cleanest single answer is the CMB rest frame. That dipole tells us the Solar System's barycenter is moving about 827,700 miles per hour relative to the CMB.[44]

Layer Earth's own orbital motion on top of that and you get a seasonal swing: when Earth's orbital velocity[45] (approximately 66,600 miles per hour) happens to align with the CMB vector, our speed in that frame is higher; when it's opposite, lower—so that the total speed varies over the year from roughly 761,000 to 894,000 miles per hour.

It is not necessary to add the Sun's galactic speed on top of the CMB speed. The CMB number already *includes* the Sun's 490,000–503,000 mile per hour orbit through the Milky Way, plus our Local Group's other tugs.[46]

---

[44] Particle Data Group, "Cosmic Microwave Background," *Review of Particle Physics* (2022): sec. 29; $v_\odot = 369.82 \pm 0.11$ km/s; $v\_LG \approx 620 \pm 15$ km/s.

[45] *Earth's Orbit*, last modified 2025, average 29.78 km/s.

[46] National Radio Astronomy Observatory (NRAO), "How long does it take the Sun to orbit the center of our galaxy?," $v \approx 225$ km/s.

For context, our Local Group's barycenter itself moves at 1.4 million miles an hour relative to the CMB, roughly toward the Hydra–Centaurus "Great Attractor" region. That's our peculiar motion atop the general expansion of space.

In regard to the concept of "moving away from the Big Bang," space seems to have no central point of expansion. Galaxies recede from each other according to Hubble's law; *we* are not flying away from a single location. Quoting speeds in the CMB frame is therefore the standard, unambiguous way to say how fast we're moving through the universe.

- While cosmology describes a gradual assembly, nothing in the observed dynamics (the speeds and balances above) *contradicts* the idea that masses and motions could have been set coherently at once; rather, the data show what combinations are required for stability.

- A neutral statement on the basic physics would be to say: Long-lived orbits require the right combination of mass distribution and initial velocities; the Sun-Earth system and the Milky Way plainly have those conditions.

THE JUGGLER AND THE SUPER-JUGGLER

Picture a street performer beneath the open sky, tossing three balls—catch, toss, catch, toss—each motion depending on the one before. That is creation as *sequence*: God speaks, light dawns; He speaks again, sky and sea divide; He speaks once more, and land rises from the deep. The beauty lies in the timing—order revealed step by step, like a master artisan laying brushstrokes on a canvas or a teacher turning pages for attentive students.

Now imagine another performer, a super-juggler of impossible skill. With one fluid motion, he sends every ball into the air at precisely the right speed, height, and angle. Their paths are perfectly coordinated, so when they reach their first peaks and begin to fall, his hands are already moving in flawless rhythm. From the very first moment, the whole performance works because the patterns were set in motion all at once.

One image portrays God as *Teacher*—the week of creation unfolding like a lesson plan, each day declaring its purpose; and culminating in Sabbath rest. The other shows God as *Sovereign Composer*—a universe so well-scored from the first

138

instant that the entire cosmic symphony plays in perfect harmony as soon as the curtain rises. Both pictures are biblical; both magnify God's wisdom. But they invite us to ponder different aspects of His creative genius: ordered progression on one hand, instantaneous coherence on the other.

THROWING THE COVER OFF THE BALL

Baseball fans know the phrase "throwing the cover off the ball," the image of a pitch launched with such force that it seems to tear itself apart. Now imagine the reverse: a ball held motionless in mid-air and then, suddenly, fired forward at full speed. The jolt would destroy the ball. Now, scale this to the cosmos.

Suppose earth were created at rest; and during the course of a "day" or two was hurled into its present velocity—spinning on its axis while racing around the sun, the sun itself orbiting the Milky Way, the galaxy rushing outward with the universe's expansion. These combined motions exceed **800,000 miles per hour**. If earth had been thrust into such speed abruptly—in merely a day or so, neither oceans nor atmosphere nor crust could have survived the violent acceleration.

Instead, the evidence suggests a cosmos already in motion from its very first moment—its forces balanced, its paths aligned, its rhythms set like notes in a score. That is not a limitation on divine power; it is a tribute to divine wisdom. Whether through a six-day unveiling or a single, sovereign command, creation itself declares a God who needs no warm-up, no trial run, no second draft. The laws of physics and the gift of life appear not as afterthoughts but as parts of one seamless act of artistry and authority.

POETIC YET TRUTHFUL READINGS OF GENESIS ONE

Augustine (4th–5th century): instantaneous creation with "seed-like principles."

In *De Genesi ad litteram*, Augustine argues that God could create all things **simul** (together / instantaneously), implanting *rationes seminales*—latent principles by which creatures unfold in time. The "six days" then mark an **order of understanding**, not a mechanical 144-hour six-day clock.[47]

---

[47] Augustine, De Genesi ad litteram (on simultaneous creation; rationes seminales). Stanford Encyclopedia of Philosophy.

Aquinas (13th century): God could create at once; six days are "fitting."

Aquinas affirms both options: God created the **substance** of things "all at once," while the six-day **distinction and adornment** is narrated to display due order and pedagogy. He explicitly says the days are assigned so that "**due order might be observed**" in instituting the world—*not* because God needs time.[48]

Framework / literary structure (20th century to present).

Meredith Kline and others see the week as a **literary framework**: Days 1 to 3 form "realms" (light/dark; sky/sea; land), Days 4 to 6 "fill" them (luminaries; birds/fish; animals/humans), culminating in the Sabbath. The pattern is **semi-poetic and architectonic**, communicating *theology* (God's kingship, vocations, worship) more than a stopwatch chronology. (Even critics agree this is the claim.)[49]

---

[48] Thomas Aquinas, Summa Theologiae I.74.2 (God could create all at once; six days are fitting to display order). New Advent.

[49] Meredith G. Kline, "Space and Time in the Genesis Cosmogony," 1996 (classic framework essay). Meredith G. Kline Resource Site.

Walton's "cosmic temple inauguration."

John H. Walton argues Genesis 1 describes **functional origins**—God assigning roles and order—framed as a **seven-day temple inauguration** in ancient Near Eastern idiom. The account is thereby "poetic" in purpose yet aims at truth about God's world as his dwelling.[50]

Jewish literary scholarship (Sarna; Alter).

Jewish exegetes often note Genesis 1's **elevated prose, parallelism, and symmetry**—a carefully composed text that teaches theology through artistry as much as through sequence. (This is not calling it "myth," but recognizing its **crafted rhetoric**.)[51]

Bottom line: Each of these proposals treats Genesis Chapter 1 as **poetic in form yet truthful in aim**—communicating who God is and what the world is *for*, not merely *how many* hours each act required.

---

[50] John H. Walton, The Lost World of Genesis One (cosmic temple inauguration; functional origins). InterVarsity Press.

[51] Nahum M. Sarna, JPS Torah Commentary: Genesis; Robert Alter, The Art of Biblical Poetry (on elevated prose/parallelism). jps.org.

THE ALL-AT-ONCE VS. THE DAY-BY-DAY CREATOR

Classical answer: Greatness is not measured by **duration** but by **sovereignty and wisdom**.

In classical theism, God could create in an instant *or* over ages; either way displays omnipotence. According to Aquinas, the multi-day ordering is **fitting** for revealing order, hierarchy, and Sabbath; for Augustine, **simultaneous** creation exalts God's transcendence over time while allowing temporal unfolding within creation. Both routes magnify God—**different facets of the same diamond.**[52]

- **The all-at-once (Super-Juggler) emphasizes**: omnipotence, foreknowledge, comprehensive coherence—the "score" written so perfectly that reality plays on cue. (The astrophysical discussion dovetails here: masses, motions, and laws must be mutually tuned from the start.)

---

[52] New Advent.

- **The day-by-day (Master Juggler) emphasizes**: pedagogy, covenantal rhythm, creaturely participation—God **teaches** by pacing, names vocations by stages, and enthrones **Sabbath** as the crown.

If we define "greater" as **raw power**, the instantaneous orchestration feels maximal. If we define "greater" as **revealed wisdom and moral pedagogy**, the six-day drama—and, by analogy, an eons-long providence—displays greater *didactic brilliance*. The **fullest** confession is: *both together*—God is great in **power** (able to create "at once") and great in **wisdom** (ordering creation to teach, to bless, to invite worship).

To the man beneath two skies, it seemed that the very atoms in our bodies were forged in the cores of ancient stars that lived and died before the sun itself was born.

To deny the antiquity of the cosmos would be to deny the testimony of the heavens themselves, as though the God who wrote Scripture had contradicted His own words by the language spoken through light and stone.

And so, some sought harmony.

CHAPTER THIRTEEN
ANCIENT EARTH AND THEOLOGY

THE GAP THEORY: A DATELESS PAST

Long before Darwin troubled theologians with evolution, geologists had already unsettled them with time. The rocks, geologists said, were far too old for Archbishop Ussher's 4004 BC creation date; the earth had stories to tell long before Eden.

Enter the "Gap Theory," first articulated in the early nineteenth century by Thomas Chalmers and later popularized in the Scofield Reference Bible. It read Genesis 1:1, *"In the beginning, God created the heavens and the earth"*—as an initial, perhaps ancient, creation.

Then came verse 2: *"The earth was without form, and void."*

Between those two verses, the theory said, lay ages untold—eons in which geological time, fossils, even catastrophes could unfold prior to the six days of Genesis; in which it was proposed that God would only then begin to order and fill the earth anew.

Scofield himself wrote in his 1909 Bible notes: *"The first creative act refers to **the dateless past**, and **gives scope for all the geologic ages.**"* (The text doesn't reveal if by, "geologic ages" Scofield intended only the Precambrian and Paleozoic; or if he meant to include the Mesozoic and Cenozoic eras as well.)

He then reads Genesis 1:2 as a judgment, which left the earth, "without form and void." Then Scofield even advises: *"Relegate fossils to **the primitive creation**, and **no conflict of science with the Genesis cosmogony remains.**"* It was a neat solution, though it satisfied few for long. Science marched on; the ages grew longer; evolution stirred controversy; and literalism dug in its heels.

THE DAY-AGE VIEW: EPOCHS, NOT HOURS

Another approach, the "Day-Age" view, read each "day" of Genesis as an "age"—a long, indefinite period in which God's creative work unfolded step by step.

Here, the sequence of Genesis roughly parallels the scientific story: light before stars, seas before land, plants before animals, humanity last of all. Each "day" spans millions or billions of years, harmonizing Scripture with modern cosmology while preserving divine purpose behind the processes.

Yet critics warned that such concordance risks bending Scripture to fit science, reshaping Genesis into a cosmic riddle solved only by modern physics. The text, they argued, speaks its own ancient language; to read modern science back into it is to mistake genre for geology.

Many major works have been written to reconcile an ancient Earth with biblical theology, particularly under the umbrella of "old-earth creationism." The following are some of the most influential works and categories of thought on this subject.

EARLY AND HISTORICAL WORKS

Reliquiae Diluvianae (1823) by William Buckland: As a respected geologist and Anglican priest, Buckland investigated geological phenomena like caves and gravel deposits to demonstrate how geological evidence aligned with the biblical account of a universal deluge.

The Pre-Adamite Earth (1846) by John Harris: This popular work among 19th-century evangelicals and others offered a version of the "gap theory," which posits a long period between Genesis 1:1 and Genesis 1:2. This allowed for an ancient Earth and fossils to exist before the six-day creation and the appearance of Adam.

The Scofield Reference Bible (1909): Although not a standalone book on theology, the highly influential footnotes in this study Bible embedded the "gap theory" into the theology of generations of conservative Protestants in the English-speaking world. The notes explicitly state that the "first creative act refers to the dateless past, and gives scope for all the geologic ages."

MODERN OLD-EARTH CREATIONISM

A Biblical Case for an Old Earth (2006) by David Snoke: This book argues that the Bible allows for an old Earth and that the young-earth position is theologically flawed. As both a scientist and a theologian, Snoke advocates for a day-age model, which interprets the "days" of creation as long, undefined periods of time.

Science, Creation and the Bible (2010) by Richard Carlson and Tremper Longman III: In this work, a physicist and a biblical scholar team up to address the conflict between modern science and the biblical creation passages. They provide a framework for reconciling the two without sacrificing either scientific or scriptural integrity.

The Genesis Flood (1961) by John C. Whitcomb and Henry M. Morris: Although known as a foundational text for modern young-earth creationism, the work was written as a response to old-earth views. The book examines the biblical and scientific implications of a global flood and served as a major point of demarcation in the creation/evolution debate.

ALBATROSS — C.W. Steinle

HERMENEUTICAL AND
LITERARY APPROACHES

The Lost World of Genesis One (2009) by John Walton: This widely influential book shifts the focus away from a literal, scientific reading of Genesis 1. Instead, Walton argues that Genesis reflects an ancient Near Eastern view of cosmology, and its purpose is to explain the functional origins of the cosmos rather than its material origins. This reframes the Genesis account so that it does not directly conflict with modern scientific findings.

Old Testament Cosmology and Divine Accommodation (2020) by John W. Hilber: Hilber's work explores the concept of "divine accommodation," arguing that God communicated with the biblical authors in terms they could understand, even if their cosmology was different from modern science. He uses Relevance Theory to disentangle the divine and human authorship of scripture.

COMPARATIVE AND MULTIPLE-VIEWPOINT BOOKS

Three Views on Creation and Evolution (2010) and *Four Views on Creation, Evolution, and Intelligent Design* (2017) edited by J.P. Moreland, John Mark Reynolds, and others: These "Counterpoints" books present different perspectives on origins, including young-earth creationism, old-earth creationism, and theistic evolution. By allowing advocates of each position to present their case and respond to critiques, the volumes provide a comprehensive overview of the different approaches Christians have taken.

CONTEMPORARY WORKS

The Language of God (2007) by Francis Collins: Written by the former director of the Human Genome Project, this book details Collins's journey from atheism to Christianity. As a committed Christian and a prominent scientist, he argues for a view of "theistic evolution," which sees evolution as the mechanism God used to create life. The book offers a firsthand account of reconciling faith and science.

COLLINS'S SYNTHESIS OF FAITH AND SCIENCE

Standing at the crossroads between science and religion, Francis Collins names his vision BioLogos—from the Greek *bios* ("life") and *logos* ("Word")—signaling a God who both authors life through His Word and sustains it through the lawful rhythms of the cosmos.[53]

For Collins, this is no retreat into "God of the gaps" theology, which Collins views as a fragile habit of invoking the divine wherever science has not yet reached. Rather, BioLogos sees God not as a stopgap in human ignorance but as the **author of the entire cosmic story**, the One who sets its laws in motion, sustains its unfolding, and grants it meaning beyond mere mechanics. Collins insists that such a view embraces the full authority of both Scripture and science without pitting them against each other.

---

[53] OPC summary of the framework structure; BioLogos overview (two-triad pattern; literary purpose). opc.org

He frames his case upon **six great premises**:

1. The universe itself began from nothing some fourteen billion years ago.

2. Its physical constants appear *fine-tuned* for life, as though expecting its arrival.

3. Life emerged—by mechanisms still mysterious—upon this stage.

4. From that point, the elegant process of evolution, operating over unimaginable epochs, produced the earth's teeming diversity without further divine "tinkering."

5. Humanity shares common ancestry with other creatures yet stands apart in moral consciousness and spiritual longing.

6. This inner life—what John Paul II called the direct creation of the soul by God— marks human beings as unique in bearing His image.

Taken together, these pillars allow Collins to affirm **both Genesis and genetics, both faith and fossils**, without twisting either into conformity with the other. The *days* of Genesis, he notes, need not be shackled to twenty-four-hour intervals any more than the Psalms' poetry should be read as meteorology; Saint Augustine himself warned against wedding Scripture to narrow interpretations that science might later overthrow.

Here Collins parts company with both **Young-Earth Creationism** and **Intelligent Design**.

The former, with its insistence upon a six-day creation mere millennia ago, not only collides with overwhelming scientific evidence but also, Collins argues, reduces the majesty of God's methods to human literalism.

The latter, though subtler, places God in the shrinking pockets of natural mystery—complexities in biology that, once explained, seem to push the Creator further into retreat. Such a deity, forever scrambling to reinsert Himself where science has not yet spoken, becomes the "clumsy God" of the gaps, rather than the sovereign author of the whole.

Against both, Collins sets BioLogos as the vision of a God whose **creative word reverberates through the lawful grandeur of the cosmos itself**—a God who "chose the elegant mechanism of evolution" as His brushstroke upon the canvas of time. In this synthesis, science and faith stand not as rival claimants to truth but as "two unshakable pillars" holding aloft the same temple of reality, each revealing what the other cannot: science the *how*, faith the *why*.[54]

Collins thus leaves his readers with a picture at once intellectually honest and spiritually luminous: a universe where quarks and quasars obey the Creator's equations, where DNA carries the signature of both history and divinity, and where the human heart, though fashioned from dust, bears the breath of God. BioLogos, he concludes, offers "by far the most scientifically consistent and spiritually satisfying" path through the modern labyrinth of belief and knowledge—one where faith need not fear the microscope, nor science the mystery of the soul.

GERALD SCHROEDER AND COSMIC TIME

One of the most intriguing modern attempts at harmony comes from Gerald Schroeder, a Jewish physicist who wields Einstein's relativity as his interpretive key.

---

[54] Francis S. Collins, *The Language of God: A Scientist Presents Evidence for Belief* (New York: Free Press, 2007), 199–208.

At the moment of the universe's birth, he notes, time itself was compressed by cosmic expansion and relativistic effects. The "clock" of the early universe ticked far faster than ours; six literal days from that frame could equal billions of years from ours. Schroeder even calculates: Day One corresponds to roughly eight billion years; Day Two, four billion; then two, one, one half, one quarter—adding up to the 13.8-billion-year age of the cosmos we measure today. Critics call this mathematical sleight of hand, noting that Genesis speaks for ancient Hebrews, not for physicists wielding Einstein's equations. Yet Schroeder insists he is not bending Scripture to fit science, but showing that science itself need not exclude the sacred.

THE ANCIENT OF DAYS

Beneath all these debates lies a deeper mystery: God Himself stands outside time altogether.

Before the first second ticked, before the first particle cooled, before "evening and morning" began to count the days, God simply *Was*. "From everlasting to everlasting, You are God," says the psalmist. The New Testament echoes: "In the beginning was the Word," not becoming, but *being*—already there before beginnings began.

Time, then, is not God's master but His creature. The ages themselves had a birth. Whether their unfolding took six days or six billion years, they all hang on the same truth: *"In the beginning, God created the heavens and the earth."*

Perhaps, in the end, Scripture was never meant to tell us the universe's age, but its Author. Genesis speaks in the language of worship, not laboratory reports. Its days may be literal, or literary, or layered with meanings we have not yet grasped. What matters is not the length of the days but the One who spoke them into being—the God who holds time itself in His hands, who enters history in Christ, who promises a future where time itself will be renewed.

For the man beneath the two skies, this means the cosmos need not be divided between science and faith, ages and angels, telescopes and theology. The heavens declare God's glory whether they are six thousand years old or fourteen billion, for their glory lies not in their age but in their Author.

As theologians, scientists, and philosophers labored across centuries to reconcile Scripture with the expanding horizons of science, the dialogue often paused at the edge of deep time.

Theories like the Gap view, the Day-Age interpretation, and even the bold proposals of thinkers like Gerald Schroeder and Francis Collins sought to unite Genesis with geology, faith with fossils, and revelation with reason. Yet questions lingered. If God authored both the Book of Scripture and the Book of Nature, what story did the rocks themselves tell?

The answers, as the next chapter will reveal, lay not in manuscripts, or in manuscripts alone, but in the silent testimony of mountains, strata, and stars—a record of ages measured not in years or centuries, but in eons written in stone.

CHAPTER FOURTEEN
THE ROCKS CRIED OUT

The man looked down and considered the Earth beneath his feet ... Not merely the soil and stone, but the great expanse of time recorded within it. Each layer, each fossil, each ripple of rock told a story far older than any written chronicle. Yet for much of human history, the age of this world was measured not in eons, but in centuries and millennia.

THE BIRTH OF GEOLOGICAL TIME

In the seventeenth century, Bishop James Ussher famously calculated that Creation occurred in 4004 BCE, based on the genealogies of the Bible. This chronology, precise to the very year, reflected the prevailing view of the time: the Earth was young, fashioned in days, its history a brief prelude to human drama. Natural history, such as it was understood, existed within the framework of Scripture. Mountains, valleys, and fossils were often attributed to a singular cataclysm—most notably Noah's Flood—rather than to the slow hand of time.

But by the late 1600s, cracks began to form in this tightly bound chronology. Niels Stensen—better known as Steno—outlined the **Principles of Stratigraphy** in 1669, observing that sedimentary layers form sequentially, with older layers buried beneath younger ones. It was a simple yet radical idea: Earth's history might be read like the pages of a book, one layer at a time.

HUTTON, SMITH, AND THE GEOLOGICAL REVOLUTION

A century later, the Scottish thinker James Hutton would carry this notion to its startling conclusion. In 1788, he presented his theory of **uniformitarianism**, arguing that the same slow processes shaping the Earth today—erosion, sedimentation, volcanic activity—had been at work for unimaginable ages. "No vestige of a beginning, no prospect of an end," he wrote, daring to suggest that Earth's history stretched back into a past too ancient for human reckoning.

William Smith, an English surveyor, added further weight to this vision when, in 1815, he produced the first geological map of Britain. He noted that layers of rock appeared in a predictable order and that fossils within them followed a sequence—

from trilobites to dinosaurs to mammals. The Earth's strata were not chaotic; they were ordered, layered, progressive. This implied deep time—an Earth far older than Ussher's tally of 6,000 years.

CATASTROPHES OR CONTINUITY?

The Cuvier–Lyell Debate

Not everyone embraced this slow, steady view of Earth's history. The French naturalist Georges Cuvier argued in the early 1800s for **catastrophism**: that sudden, violent events—great floods or upheavals—had shaped the planet. Some saw in his ideas a scientific echo of biblical cataclysms.

But Charles Lyell, building on Hutton's work, challenged this notion in his *Principles of Geology* (1830s). He demonstrated that slow, consistent forces—not singular catastrophes—were enough to explain mountains rising, rivers carving valleys, and fossils entombed over ages. His work profoundly influenced the young Charles Darwin, who would soon contemplate the implications of deep time for the evolution of life itself.

DISCOVERING DEEP TIME

As the nineteenth century progressed, the **geologic column** took shape: Precambrian, Paleozoic, Mesozoic, Cenozoic—eras spanning hundreds of millions of years. Fossils were no longer mere curiosities; they were timekeepers, marking the passage of ages in stone.

Then, at the dawn of the twentieth century, a revolution occurred. The discovery of **radioactivity** by Henri Becquerel in 1896, followed by the work of Ernest Rutherford and Bertram Boltwood, allowed scientists to measure the age of rocks using radioactive decay. By the mid-1900s, radiometric dating had pushed the Earth's age back not thousands, but **billions** of years—to around 4.54 billion, as modern methods now confirm.

THE MODERN SYNTHESIS

A Planet Written in Many Scripts

The twentieth century brought a flood of corroborating evidence. **Plate tectonics** revealed continents drifting over hundreds of millions of years. **Ice cores** from Greenland and Antarctica preserved climate records stretching back hundreds of thousands of years. **Seafloor sediments** charted ocean and climate changes over millions of years, while **tree rings** offered precise annual records extending thousands of years into the past.

Today, these independent methods—radiometric, stratigraphic, paleontological, astronomical—all converge on a single conclusion: the Earth is ancient beyond ordinary comprehension, its story written across billions of years. Each line of evidence corroborates the others, dismantling any lingering notion of a world created in recent millennia.

PLATE TECTONICS

The theory of plate tectonics stands as one of the most transformative developments in Earth science. Formally synthesized in the 1960s, plate tectonics unified a variety of disparate geological observations—continental drift, sea-floor spreading, earthquake distribution—into a coherent model explaining how Earth's lithosphere is partitioned and in motion.

Imagine Earth's outer shell, the lithosphere, broken into a mosaic of massive plates. These plates—ranging from the enormous Pacific Plate to smaller ones like the Nazca—float atop the more ductile asthenosphere. Driven by convective currents in the underlying mantle, these plates drift, collide, slide past one another, and in doing so sculpt the planet's surface.

Evidence for this grand-scale movement emerged from multiple directions. First, the jigsaw-like fit of continental coastlines—particularly the matching of South America's bulge to Africa's gulf—had long intrigued early geologists. Fossil records provided deeper clues: identical fossils of certain Mesosaurus reptiles found both in South America and southwestern Africa implied that these continents were indeed once joined.

Mid-20th-century oceanic surveys brought a seismic breakthrough: mapping of the ocean floor revealed a central ridge system—the mid-ocean ridges—radiating like seams across the oceans. Symmetrical magnetic striping on either side of these ridges captured the story of Earth's magnetic field reversing at regular intervals; as molten rock emerged at these ridges and cooled, it preserved magnetic orientations. This "tape-measure" of magnetic anomalies showed that new crust was continuously added at ridges and pushed outward, confirming the reality of sea-floor spreading.

Earthquakes trace the boundaries where plates interact. Subduction zones—where one plate plunges beneath another—spawn the deepest quakes and sculpt volcanic arcs like the Andes or the Cascades. Transform faults, places where plates grind past each other laterally, give us the San Andreas system in California. These global patterns of seismicity, along with the age distribution of oceanic crust (young at ridges, older farther away), confirmed that the Earth is actively renewing its surface over tremendous timescales.

Thus, plate tectonics not only explained the dynamic movements of continents and ocean basins, but also underscored that these processes require deep time—tens to hundreds of millions of years—to effect such sweeping changes.

ICE CORES

Next, let's journey into the polar ice caps, where ancient layers of frozen water have serenely recorded Earth's climate through the ages. Ice cores—long cylinders of ice drilled from places like Greenland and Antarctica—are among the most precise climate archives in existence.

Each year, snowfall compresses older snow beneath it, forming a new layer of ice. Over thousands of years these layers accumulate in a simple, readable sequence—a natural calendar of past climate. Embedded within are tiny air bubbles, each preserving a snapshot of the atmosphere at the time the snow fell—its temperature, and levels of nitrogen, oxygen, carbon dioxide, and other gases.

By extracting cores that extend hundreds of thousands of years, scientists have read fluctuations in carbon dioxide and methane, directly matching them with shifts in temperature. The rhythmic alternation of glacial and interglacial periods— cycles of cold then warm—is clearly outlined, driven by Earth's long-term orbital variations known as Milankovitch cycles.

Further richness emerges through stable isotopes of oxygen (delta-18O) and hydrogen (delta-D)[55] in the water molecules, which serve as proxies for past temperatures: heavier isotopic ratios correlate with warmer periods. Through layer counting, trapped gases, volcanic ash layers, and annual cycles (like

---

[55] The stable hydrogen isotope ratio of deuterium to protium.

seasonal melt layers), researchers chart back climate changes over 800,000 years (in Antarctica) or around 125,000 years (in Greenland) with remarkable resolution.

These records span far beyond human history, bridging ice ages and warm interludes. The consistency across multiple cores from different locations—for example, confirming global minima during ice ages—further attests to their reliability. In effect, ice cores provide both a timeline and a temperature record, demonstrating profound, long-term variability in Earth's climate—something that simply doesn't align with a 6,000-year-old Earth model.

SEAFLOOR SEDIMENTS

Delving beneath the oceans, we encounter another vast archive: marine sediments. Though the seafloor is partially renewed through spreading, sediment layers can still reach meters to tens of meters in depth, layered over millions of years.

As organisms die in the ocean, their remains settle toward the bottom, forming ooze composed of calcium carbonate or silica, depending on the dominant microfossils.[56] Coupled with inputs of terrestrial dust, volcanic ash, and chemical precipitates, these sediments create stratified records across marine basins.

Scientists retrieve cores from the seafloor that preserve continuous depositional histories. Within these layers, paleontologists and geochemists examine microfossil assemblages and stable isotopes, key indicators of past ocean conditions and climate.

One oft-used measure is the ratio of oxygen isotopes ($\delta^{18}O$ again), recorded in the shells of foraminifera, which reflects global ice volume and deep-water temperatures. Over alternations of glacial-interglacial cycles, the sea record charts the waxing and waning of ice sheets and affirms orbital-paced climate changes.

The depth-age relationship in such cores is calibrated using multiple techniques: biostratigraphy (fossil succession), paleomagnetic reversals, radiometric dating of volcanic ash layers (tephra), and even astrochronology (matching

---

[56] e.g., foraminifera, diatoms.

sediment layering to Earth's orbital cycles). Some deep-sea cores encompass several million years of time, revealing patterns in biodiversity, carbon cycling, and ocean chemistry.

Through these studies marine sediment cores show that Earth has experienced many distinct climate regimes—glaciations, warm periods, ocean acidifications, ecosystem shifts—spanning tens of millions of years. Such evidence discloses an old and fluctuating planet.

TREE RINGS

Turning landward again, trees offer their own annual ledger of history: dendrochronology, the science of tree-ring dating.

A tree adds a ring for each growing season—usually one per year in temperate climates. Variations in ring width reflect environmental stressors: wider rings typically indicate favorable growing conditions (warm, wet growing seasons), while narrow rings suggest drought, cold, or other challenges.

By overlapping ring-width patterns from living trees with those from older, preserved wood—whether dead standing trees, buried logs, or historic artifacts—scientists build extended timelines that can stretch back thousands of years. For example, bristlecone pines from the White Mountains of California provide ring records that go back over 9,000 years. By carefully crossdating patterns of wide and narrow rings among multiple trees, researchers assemble continuous chronologies that stretch across millennia.

These chronologies are then used to calibrate radiocarbon dating and study climate change on annual and decadal scales. The fidelity of the record—down to individual years—allows reconstruction of short-lived anomalies (volcanic eruptions, droughts), as well as longer trends.

Importantly, tree-ring sequences from different regions interlock to form larger regional records, reinforcing the continuity and precise chronology. These reliable annual records stand in sharp contrast to the idea that Earth has only existed for a few thousand years.

MULTIPLE METHODS AND CONVERGENCE

Finally, the most compelling affirmation of Earth's deep time comes from the convergence of these multiple, independent dating methods—each based on different physics, chemistry, and natural processes—yet pointing to the same conclusion: Earth is billions of years old.

Radiometric dating uses radioactive decay chains (like uranium 238 to lead 206, or potassium 40 to argon 40), each with known half-lives. When scientists date the oldest known Earth minerals (zircons from Western Australia), ages reach approximately 4.4 billion years. Meteorites, considered to have formed around the same time as the solar system, date at about 4.56 billion years. These results consistently affirm Earth's antiquity and the shared origin of the solar system.

Isochron dating, **luminescence dating**, **argon to argon dating**, and **cosmogenic nuclide dating** offer cross-checks and refine dates for rock formation, sediment burial, and surface exposure, over timescales ranging from thousands to billions of years.

The brilliance lies in cross-validation: radiometric dating matches stratigraphic succession, which matches fossil evolution, which matches paleomagnetic sequences, which matches ice-core chronologies, and so on. When all these independent lines of evidence overlap—despite being grounded in different physical principles—they reinforce confidence in the ages they reveal.

In tandem, these methods dismantle any reasonable case for a recently created Earth that was inhabited long ago. Instead, they establish a coherent, multilayered, and consistent picture of an Earth shaped over billions of years by slow, observable processes.

Taken together, these show how modern scientific methods—ranging from plate tectonics to tree rings—collectively construct a robust narrative of Earth's immense age. Each approach, whether through the grand motion of continents, the frozen archives of ice, the layers of ocean sediments, the growth rings of trees, or the cross-validated dating methods, reinforces the "astronomical" timescales required to build our world as we know it.

The next chapter will descend from galaxies and epochs to the mystery of *ourselves*—of consciousness, morality, and the human soul. For even if the stars are ancient and the earth old, we remain creatures of dust and breath, image-bearers in whom matter and spirit meet.

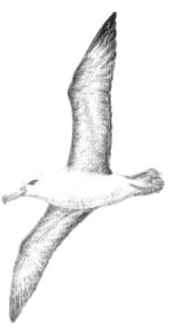

CHAPTER FIFTEEN
THE SOUL AND THE
IMAGE OF GOD

The man beneath the two skies looked inward...

For he had heard the story told by the first sky—
that human beings are but clever animals, accidents
of chemistry, temporary arrangements of atoms
destined to dissolve when the universe grows cold.
He had heard the story told by the second sky—that
humanity bears the *imago Dei*, the image of God,
that beneath flesh and bone lies something eternal,
something not explained by stardust alone.

Between these two stories lay the weight of a
question:

What is man, that Thou art mindful of him?[57]

---

[57] Psalm 8:4.

MATTER AND MIND

Materialism insists that mind emerges from matter the way steam rises from boiling water: give the universe enough time, enough atoms, enough blind collisions, and eventually self-awareness appears. Thoughts, it says, are chemical signals; emotions are evolutionary adaptations; morality is the inheritance of tribal instincts polished by natural selection.

Yet consciousness refuses to fit neatly inside this box.

For the physical sciences can describe the brain's mechanisms in exquisite detail—the neurons firing, the synapses connecting, the electrical pulses sparking like city lights at night—but no description of circuits and chemistry explains the *experience* of being alive, the inner world of thoughts and dreams and moral conviction.

Philosophers call this the "hard problem" of consciousness: why should atoms arranged in a certain way produce not merely reactions, but awareness? Why should matter wake up and say *I*?

If the universe is nothing but particles in motion, how does it give rise to poetry and prayer, to grief and love, to hope for eternity?

THE IMAGE OF GOD

The ancient Scriptures speak with startling simplicity: "God created man in His own image... male and female He created them."

What this "image" means has filled libraries with debate. Some see it in human rationality, others in morality; others in our capacity for relationship, creativity, or dominion over the earth. Perhaps it lies in all of these, perhaps in something deeper still—the mystery of personhood itself, the human being as a creature of both dust and breath, body and spirit, earth and heaven.

Whatever its precise meaning, the imago Dei tells us this: human beings are not cosmic accidents. We are not mere clever mammals scribbling equations on a doomed planet circling an indifferent star. We are creatures addressed by God, known by God, bearing in our very existence a reflection of the One who spoke the galaxies into being.

THE MORAL DIMENSION

Materialism struggles here as well. If the universe is indifferent, if evolution selects only for survival, then morality itself becomes a curious by-product—a set of instincts useful for keeping one's genes alive, nothing more.

But the human conscience refuses to cooperate. Across centuries and cultures, people have believed that some things are truly right and others truly wrong—that love is better than hatred, that courage is better than cowardice, that justice is better than cruelty. We argue about *what* is right and wrong because we assume there is something real to argue about.

C.S. Lewis noted that to call a river crooked, one must have some idea of a straight line. To call an action evil, one must have some idea of the good. If morality were merely a trick of evolution, we might feel impulses toward cooperation or self-preservation, but we would not speak of *ought* and *ought not*, of justice and guilt, of conscience and moral law.[58]

---

[58] Mere Christianity, "The Rival Conceptions of God".

The very language of right and wrong suggests a Law above biology, a Voice above instinct.

THE LONGING FOR ETERNITY

Then there is the longing itself.

Humans dream of immortality, write epics about paradise, ponder the afterlife, and grieve as though death were an intruder rather than a natural fact. "God has set eternity in the human heart," wrote the author of Ecclesiastes.[59] Even those who deny God often speak as though love and justice deserve some permanence, as though beauty and meaning ought not to vanish when the neurons stop firing.

Where do such longings come from? Evolutionary biology can speak of survival instincts, psychology of wish-fulfillment, neurology of electrical impulses—but none explains why beings in a temporary, accidental universe should so stubbornly desire the spiritual and eternal.

---

[59] Ecclesiastes 3:11

The Christian answer is simple and staggering: because we were made for it. We are creatures of time with souls for whom time will not be enough.

THE RESURRECTION AND HUMAN DESTINY

The New Testament ties all these threads together—the mystery of consciousness, the image of God, the longing for eternity—in the Resurrection of Christ.

If Christ rose from the dead, then humanity's story is not decay toward oblivion but renewal toward glory. The soul's worth is confirmed, the body's future is secured, the image of God in humanity is not erased by death but restored by grace.

Here is the difference between the two skies: the first tells of stardust become consciousness, destined to fall silent; the second tells of dust shaped into living souls, destined for resurrection because Christ has passed through death and opened the way beyond it.

TOWARD A THEOLOGY
OF THE HUMAN PERSON

The man beneath the two skies begins to see:

- He is not merely an organism solving chemical equations but a creature bearing God's image.
- His conscience points to a moral law deeper than instinct.
- His longing for eternity whispers of a destiny beyond the grave.
- His reason, his love, his creativity, his grief—all speak of a mystery too large for atoms alone.

To speak of the human soul, then, is not to retreat from science but to insist that science alone cannot tell the whole story. The universe may be vast, the stars ancient, the galaxies innumerable—but the human person stands at the intersection of dust and divinity, matter and meaning, creation and Creator.

The next chapter will lift our eyes once more from the human person to the cosmos itself, asking whether faith can embrace the grandeur of a universe fourteen billion years wide without fear, and whether science can speak of that grandeur without closing the door on transcendence.

CHAPTER SIXTEEN
FAITH AND THE COSMOS

The man beneath the two skies looked outward once more...

He had pondered the age of the universe, the question of miracles, the mystery of the human soul. Now the stars themselves seemed to call for an answer. For the night sky spoke in light-years and redshifts, in galaxies colliding and stars collapsing, in cosmic background radiation from the dawn of time. Yet Scripture spoke of the heavens declaring the glory of God, of creation groaning for redemption, of Christ holding all things together.

Could one vision contain both—the cold mathematics of the cosmos and the warmth of divine purpose? Could faith lift its eyes to a universe fourteen billion years wide without shrinking back in fear?

THE UNIVERSE AS CREATION, NOT CHAOS

Modern cosmology tells of a universe with a beginning: a singularity, an expansion, galaxies forming, stars igniting, planets spinning out from stellar debris. Physics measures it in equations; astronomy photographs it in breathtaking detail; chemistry traces our very bodies to the "furnaces" of ancient stars.

But the Bible had long spoken of a universe with a beginning: *"In the beginning, God created the heavens and the earth."*

To the ancient world, this was a staggering claim. Pagan myths often pictured chaos as eternal, with the gods themselves emerging from its darkness. Genesis dared to say that chaos had not the last word—that before matter or energy or time itself, there was God, eternal and free, speaking creation into existence.

Modern cosmology, in its own way, agrees: time, space, matter—all had a beginning. The difference lies in whether that beginning was personal or impersonal, whether the universe sprang from blind necessity or from divine purpose.

THE SCOPE OF REDEMPTION

Christian faith has often spoken of salvation in personal terms—souls forgiven, lives transformed, individuals reconciled to God. Yet Scripture also speaks cosmically:

- Paul writes of "all things" being reconciled through Christ, "whether on earth or in heaven."
- Isaiah foretells a new heavens and a new earth.
- Revelation ends with creation itself renewed, not discarded, the dwelling of God among His people on a redeemed earth beneath redeemed skies.

The Incarnation thus links heaven and earth, Creator and creation, eternity and time. The Word became flesh not to rescue us *from* creation, but to redeem creation itself.

FEAR AND WONDER IN THE MODERN AGE

For many the age and depth and breadth of the cosmos inspires not faith but fear. How small we seem against galaxies whose light began its journey before humanity existed! How brief our lives beside stars that burn for billions of years! How fragile our planet in a universe expanding toward an inevitable heat death!

And yet, the psalmist looked at the same night sky— far smaller in his eyes than in ours—and asked, *"What is man that You are mindful of him?"* He did not despair. He marveled. For the heavens that dwarfed him also declared the glory of the One who made both stars and souls. Modern science can deepen that wonder rather than diminish it. To learn that the elements in our bodies were forged in stellar furnaces, that the photons striking our eyes began their journey before Abraham walked the earth, that the laws of physics are fine-tuned to permit life—all this need not exile God from the cosmos. It can instead enlarge our vision of His majesty.

Where Earth Fits into the Universe

The man couldn't help but wonder if mankind was alone in such an unfathomable universe. Perhaps the heavens were barren, or perhaps life bloomed unseen in corners of the cosmos beyond any signal or voyage. Either way, the vastness above seemed to demand reverence, as though the silence itself were a canvas stretched by the Creator to invite both faith and inquiry.

The story of the cosmos invites a question as old as wonder itself: *Are we alone?* For centuries, astronomy has been driven by measurements of what is "out there"—the distances to the stars, the structure of the galaxies, the age of the universe. But once the telescope became powerful enough to find worlds beyond our solar system, speculation turned into cautious probability. How many planets exist in the universe? And what might that mean for life?

Modern astronomy now suggests that planets are not rare ornaments of a few privileged stars. They appear to be the norm. Surveys such as NASA's **Kepler** mission have revealed thousands of exoplanets and from these discoveries astronomers estimate that **on average, every star in the Milky Way hosts at least one planet**—many have more. If our galaxy contains some **200 billion stars**, as current estimates propose, that means **200 billion planets** right here in the Milky Way alone.

How Many "Worlds" in the Milky Way?

Scale this to the **observable universe**, which may contain 10^{22} **to** 10^{24} **stars**, and the number of planets quickly dwarfs human imagination. Even when restricting the count to "Earth-sized" worlds in the so-called habitable zone, the tally for the Milky Way alone runs to the **tens of billions**. In sheer numbers, planets abound.

But numbers alone do not answer the deeper question of life. To frame that puzzle, astronomer Frank Drake in 1961 proposed what has become known as the **Drake Equation**—a way of breaking the unknown into a series of smaller, uncertain steps. The equation multiplies factors such as the rate of star formation, the fraction of stars with planets, the number of potentially habitable planets per star, the fraction where life actually begins, the fraction where intelligence arises, the fraction that develops detectable technology, and finally the **lifetime of such civilizations** before they vanish or fall silent.

Each term hides vast ignorance: we have only one known example—Earth—for many of these factors. Adjust the numbers optimistically; and the galaxy could be teeming with civilizations. Choose conservatively; and Earth might be utterly alone. The Drake Equation does not give an answer so much as a structured way to admit how little we know.

The Fermi Paradox

And so arises what physicists call the **Fermi Paradox**. If the universe is so old, so vast, and so richly endowed with planets, then—*as physicist Enrico Fermi asked over lunch in 1950*, "Where is everybody?" Why no signals, no visitors, no artifacts drifting through space?

Some scientists suggest we have simply not searched deeply enough. Others suspect what is called the **Great Filter**: perhaps life rarely advances past microbial forms, or intelligence often destroys itself before reaching the stars. Another view holds that civilizations may exist but choose not to broadcast, or that cosmic distances render contact hopeless. More sobering still, perhaps intelligent life has flickered and perished many times across cosmic history, leaving no trace for us to find.

The tension between the **statistical expectation** of abundant life and the **silence of the skies** remains unresolved. Yet both the equation and the paradox sharpen our sense of Earth's place. Whether life beyond us is common or rare, the one world we *know* to be alive—the thin biosphere clinging to this small blue planet—becomes all the more astonishing against the backdrop of a silent universe.

189

ALBATROSS — C.W. Steinle

FAITH LARGE ENOUGH FOR GALAXIES

Too often faith has feared science, as though God were a rival hypothesis needing "gaps" to hide in. But the God of Scripture is no mere explanation among others; He is the ground of all explanations, the Author of nature's laws and the freedom behind them.

To say, "God created" is not to compete with cosmology over mechanisms; it is to confess that behind every mechanism lies meaning. Gravity explains how the planets move; it does not explain why there is a cosmos at all, nor why the cosmos is ordered, intelligible, and capable of bearing life that can ponder its own existence.

When faith shrinks before science, it forgets its own story. The God who spoke through prophets and apostles also speaks through galaxies and genomes, through quarks and quasars, through the very rationality of the universe itself.

The Unity of Truth

Christian thinkers through the centuries—Augustine, Aquinas, Kepler, Newton—have insisted on the unity of truth. "All truth is God's truth," they said, whether written in Scripture or discovered in nature.

Reframing the Agedness of the Cosmos

- The voice of Revelation asserts, "Thou art worthy, O Lord, to receive glory and honour and power: for thou hast created all things, and for thy pleasure they are and were created."[60]
- God exists before and outside of time.
- The longer the time creation has existed (perhaps 13.8 billion years), the greater the God who stands outside of time—thus God's flattering designation as "The Ancient of Days."[61]

Conflict arises only when we confuse levels of explanation, when we demand that Genesis speak like a physics textbook or that physics pronounce on metaphysics. Science describes the patterns of creation; theology speaks of the Creator's purposes. The two are not enemies unless we make them so.

As Galileo, accused of heresy for studying the heavens, once wrote, "The Bible tells us how to go to heaven, not how the heavens go."

---

[60] Revelation 4:11 (KJV).

[61] Daniel 7:9-22.

CHRIST AT THE CENTER

The New Testament dares to place Christ not only at the center of redemption but also at the center of creation itself:

- *"Through Him all things were made; without Him nothing was made that has been made."*
- *"In Him all things hold together."*
- *"The Son is the radiance of God's glory... sustaining all things by His powerful word."*

If this is true, then the galaxies are not godless; the laws of physics are not ultimate; the vastness of space does not exile humanity from meaning. Christ stands at the heart of it all, the Logos through whom the universe exists and toward whom it moves.

TOWARD A COSMIC FAITH

The man beneath the two skies begins to see a larger horizon:

- A faith too small for the cosmos will wither before the telescope.
- A science too narrow for transcendence will wither before the human spirit.

- But a vision in which Christ holds together creation and redemption, galaxies and grace, law and miracle, matter and meaning—this vision can bear the weight of both skies.

Such a faith does not fear the universe's age, or size or complexity. It stands beneath the stars and worships the One who calls them by name—and who also calls each human soul by name!

The next chapter will bring these threads toward resolution, asking whether the tension between science and faith must remain an albatross at all—or whether a greater synthesis awaits, one in which the two skies speak together rather than against each other.

CHAPTER SEVENTEEN
LIFTING THE ALBATROSS

The man beneath the two skies had carried the weight for so long he had almost forgotten what it was like to stand upright.

On one side stretched the universe as science told it: vast, ancient, governed by laws so elegant they could be written in mathematics, so indifferent they gave no hint of purpose. It seemed a closed system, a silent cathedral where no voice from beyond ever spoke.

On the other side rang the story of faith: a God who made the heavens and the earth, who entered history through prophets and apostles, through the Incarnation and the Resurrection, who promised a new creation when all things would be made right.

For centuries, the man had been told these skies could not coexist—that he must choose between faith and reason, Bible and telescope, miracles and mathematics, Christ and cosmology.

He had believed them. The burden of divided loyalties weighed like iron across his shoulders.

But what if the weight itself was the illusion?

THE FALSE CHOICE

Modern thought has often painted science and faith as rival empires at war over the same territory. If science explains the rainbow through refraction, there is no need for covenantal promises; if geology speaks of ages before Adam, Genesis must be legend; if biology traces life through evolution, the Creator must retreat into myth.

Yet this is a false choice.

Explaining *how* rainbows form does not answer *why* there is beauty at all, nor why the laws of physics are so precisely ordered that light itself obeys equations elegant enough to predict their own results. Science maps the mechanics of reality; faith speaks to its meaning, its origin, its ultimate destiny. The albatross hangs heavy only when we confuse these questions—when we demand that science pronounce on miracles, or that Scripture teach cosmology, as though Genesis had been written in the language of particle physics rather than the poetry of creation.

HARMONY, NOT HOSTILITY

The early scientists—the Keplers, the Newtons, the Pascals—never imagined they were undermining faith by studying the natural world. To them, the universe was a book written in two languages: Scripture and nature, revelation and reason. To read one was not to silence the other.

Kepler, after mapping the motion of the planets, wrote that he was "thinking God's thoughts after Him." Newton, formulating the laws of motion and gravitation, filled his notebooks with biblical commentary. Faraday, father of electromagnetism, called the natural world "a divine manuscript."

It was only later that some began treating science as a rival to faith rather than its ally, as though discovering gravity meant there was no God to hold the stars in place, or learning about evolution meant life had no Author.

But gravity does not replace God. Evolution does not erase providence. The Big Bang does not banish creation. They tell us how the story unfolds; they do not write the story themselves.

THE ROLE OF MIRACLES

Here, too, the weight lifts when we see miracles not as violations of nature but as revelations of its Author.

The Incarnation, the Resurrection, the signs and wonders of Scripture—they do not declare nature meaningless, but meaningful; not lawless, but open to the One whose laws serve His purposes. If the universe is a poem, miracles are the capital letters, the places where the Author emphasizes His presence in history. A closed universe has no room for such acts. But a created universe is never closed. It exists because God wills it, sustains it, and calls it toward redemption.

TIME, AGES AND THE ANCIENT OF DAYS

The debates over creation days, cosmic time, evolution, and geology have often carried "more heat than light."[62] Must the days of Genesis be literal twenty-four-hour periods? Must the universe be six thousand years old or fourteen billion? Must creation and evolution be sworn enemies?

---

[62] Reversal and play on words from Hamlet Act I, Scene III.

Scripture itself invites deeper reflection. Before the sun marks the first day, before Adam walks the earth, before time itself begins to tick, God simply *IS*. The "Ancient of Days" stands outside hours and ages alike.

Whether the cosmos unfolded in six days or six billion years, its meaning rests not in the length of its timeline but in the Lord of its history.

THE CROSS AND THE COSMOS

Christian faith dares to say that the One through whom galaxies came into being entered His own creation, walked its soil, wept its tears, and bore its sin. The Logos who spoke light into darkness became flesh beneath Ancient Roman rule; was crucified under Pontius Pilate, and rose on the third day as the first fruits of a new creation.

Here science falls silent, not because it is refuted but because it is limited. Telescopes can photograph the edges of the observable universe, but they cannot measure grace. Microscopes can peer into the cell's machinery, but they cannot explain love strong enough to endure death on a cross for the world's redemption.

The Cross stands as the axis of both skies, the place where the Author enters His own story to bring it toward its promised restoration.

The man saw that science need not deny faith, that faith need not fear science, that the God of Genesis is not threatened by galaxies, that the Christ of Calvary is not eclipsed by cosmology, that miracles are not embarrassments, but signs; that time itself serves eternity.

The heavens told of hydrogen and helium, of galaxies and gravity—and the psalmist still sang, *"The heavens declare the glory of God."*

The Scriptures told of creation and covenant, of Incarnation and Resurrection—and the scientist could still marvel at the rational beauty of the cosmos without closing the door on transcendence.

Both skies met in Christ, the One in whom all things hold together.

The stars still burned. The Scriptures still spoke.

The questions of: time and evolution, of miracles and meaning, of science and faith, had not all been solved. But the burden of rivalry had lifted, and in its place stood wonder.

CHAPTER EiGHTEEN
THE SYMPHONY OF THE SKiES

The man stood once more beneath the two skies…

He had walked a long road.

Through the first sky had come prophets and promises, apocalyptic visions and eschatological fears. It had thundered of judgment, spoken in trumpet blasts of the end, painted pictures of fire and finality. It had called men to repentance with the urgency of a world rushing toward its last breath.

Daniel spoke of thrones set in place and the Ancient of Days taking His seat; Matthew recorded Christ warning of sun and moon darkened, of stars falling from the heavens; Revelation unfolded visions of seals and trumpets and bowls of wrath poured upon the earth.

ALBATROSS — C.W. Steinle

Through the second sky had come telescopes and test tubes, astronomers and atoms, biologists and billion-year timelines. It whispered of impersonal forces, of galaxies without number, of a universe vast beyond measure and silent beyond comfort.

Hubble found the galaxies racing apart; Penzias and Wilson heard the faint microwave echo of cosmic birth; Darwin traced the branching tree of life through eons of natural selection; Freud reduced faith to wish-fulfillment; Nietzsche announced the death of God and the dawn of modern man.

For so long, the man beneath these skies felt pulled apart, as though he must choose between one vision or the other—between faith and reason, between hope and honesty, between miracle and mechanism.

One sky told him the world was ending; the other told him it never had meaning in the first place.

And so, he had carried that weight.

THE ALBATROSS OF FEAR

The first sky's burden was fear—the fear that history was a slow march toward apocalypse, that every war and rumor of war signaled the final trumpet, that science and progress were mere illusions before the approaching storm.

Here lay the weight of those who read every earthquake as divine warning, every headline as prophecy—every generation as the last. The heavens themselves became instruments of dread: the moon darkened, the stars fell, the sun withheld its light.

Centuries of voices joined this chorus: millennialists in the Early Church expecting Christ's reign after six thousand years of human history; medieval mystics like Joachim of Fiore predicting the dawn of the "Age of the Spirit"; the Millerites gathering in 1844 for a return that never came; modern prophecy teachers pointing to Israel's rebirth in 1948 as the "super-sign" of the last days, echoing Scofield's famous Bible notes linking Genesis 12:3 and Ezekiel 37 to twentieth-century events.

Beneath that sky, the man felt the weight of doom pressing down, as though hope itself were forbidden until the final reckoning burned the earth clean.

THE ALBATROSS OF DOUBT

The second sky's burden was different.

Here there was no doom, only indifference. No judgment, only silence. The stars wheeled above, galaxies collided, comets traced their long ellipses around the sun—all without meaning, all without message.

Darwin spoke of blind selection shaping life through chance and survival alone. Freud diagnosed religion as a projection of human longings. Marx dismissed it as the "opium of the people." Nietzsche thundered that God was dead, and with Him the transcendent source of truth and morality.

The modern age told the man that the universe had no voice but his own, no Author, no Logos, no purpose beyond survival and reproduction.

Here lay the weight of reduction: miracles dismissed as superstition, morality as tribal instinct, consciousness as chemical reaction, love itself as a trick played by selfish genes on fragile minds.

Beneath that sky, the man felt the weight of meaninglessness pressing down, as though transcendence itself had been erased from the dictionary of existence.

THE MEETING OF THE SKIES

But as the man stood beneath both heavens, he began to see what he had not seen before.

The two skies were not enemies. They were estranged brothers, each holding half the truth, each distorted when taken alone.

The first sky was right to say history has direction—that the world groans for redemption, that human lives bear eternal weight. But it was wrong when it shrank the future to fear, when it confused hope with doom, when it turned promise into panic.

The second sky was right to marvel at the cosmos, to trace its laws, to celebrate reason and discovery. But it was wrong when it declared transcendence an illusion, when it mistook mechanism for meaning, when it reduced wonder to mere chemistry in motion.

The albatross was slipping from his shoulders, not because the questions vanished, but because the false opposition had. The skies were not rivals after all. They were two witnesses, speaking in different tongues, declaring the same glory.

Both skies were true in what they affirmed; both were false in what they denied.

THE CROSS AT THE CENTER

For the Scriptures spoke of a Christ who was there before the first light broke across the void, "In the beginning was the Word... Through Him all things were made; without Him nothing was made that has been made."[63]

They spoke of a Logos, a Word behind both the laws of nature and the covenants of promises, a Wisdom through whom galaxies and atoms, angels and animals, space-time and human souls came into being.[64]

---

[63] John 1:1–3.

[64] Colossians 1:15–17; Hebrews 1:2–3.

They spoke of a Cross planted in real history, yet reaching outward to cosmic dimensions—reconciling, Paul dared to say, "all things, whether on earth or in heaven."[65]

They spoke of a Resurrection not only as miracle but also as first fruits of a new creation, the pledge that, "Neither doom nor meaninglessness would write the final chapter!"

At the center of both skies stood Christ:

- The Creator behind the cosmos of the scientists.
- The Redeemer behind the hopes of the prophets.
- The One in whom *all things hold together.*

LIFTING THE ALBATROSS

And the man felt the weight being lifted.

For he saw, that faith need not fear science; the God of Genesis was not dethroned by galaxies or genomes. He saw that science need not scorn faith—that the rational beauty of the cosmos

---

whispered of purpose, not absurdity. Gerald Schroeder's work on relativity suggested that the six "days" of creation could be measured in cosmic time as billions of years, collapsing the war between Genesis and geology.

C.S. Lewis reminded the modern world that to "see through" everything is the same as not to see at all—that naturalism undermines even the reason by which it seeks to disprove transcendence.

The man saw that miracles were not embarrassments to be explained away, nor scientific laws enemies to be overthrown. Both were music played by the same Composer—one the steady rhythm of natural order, the other the soaring melody of divine action, each meaningful in its own way.

He saw that time itself, whether in days or billions of years, was the stage on which God wrote His story—a story rushing not toward annihilation but toward resurrection, not toward despair but toward renewal.

ONE SKY AT LAST

The man lifted his eyes once more.

The two skies were still there: one telling of galaxies and gravity, the other of grace and glory. But they no longer pulled against each other. They arched together now over a single creation, a single history, a single hope.

The psalmist's words came alive: *"The heavens declare the glory of God; the skies proclaim the work of His hands. Day after day they pour forth speech; night after night they display knowledge."*[66] Paul's words echoed: *"For since the creation of the world God's invisible qualities—His eternal power and divine nature— have been clearly seen, being understood from what has been made."*[67]

The heavens declared the glory of God through both telescope and text, through reason and revelation, through quarks and quasars, through prophets and apostles.

---

[66] Psalm 19:1–2.

[67] Romans 1:20.

ALBATROSS — C.W. Steinle

The same Christ who entered history beneath one sky now reigns over both, holding together the laws of physics and the promises of Scripture, the silence of space and the songs of the redeemed.

The man beneath the two skies finally understood:

He did not have to choose between faith and science, between wonder and worship, between reason and revelation.

For the Author of one sky had written the other as well.

And so, the book closes not with the ending of history, but with the opening of possibility.

The albatross has taken flight.

The man walks on.

And the two skies above him, at last, belong to the same God.

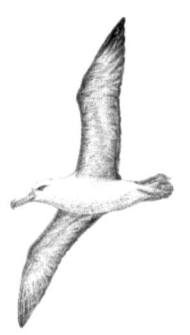

END NOTES AND BIOGRAPHY

Bibliography

Abanes, Richard. *End-Time Visions: The Road to Armageddon?* New York: Four Walls Eight Windows, 1998.

Alvarez, Luis W., Walter Alvarez, Frank Asaro, Helen V. Michel, and Peter Claeys. "Extraterrestrial Cause for the Cretaceous-Tertiary Extinction." *Science* 208, no. 4448 (1980): 1095–1108.

Augustine. *De Genesi ad litteram.* Stanford Encyclopedia of Philosophy. Accessed 2025.

Bardeen, Charles, et al. "On the Radiative Forcing of Stratospheric Soot Aerosols." *Journal of Geophysical Research: Atmospheres* 122, no. 9 (2017): 4326–49.

Bickerman, Elias. *Chronology of the Ancient World.* Ithaca, NY: Cornell University Press, 1988.

BioLogos. "Overview of the Two-Triad Pattern and Literary Purpose." OPC.org. Accessed 2025.

Boyer, Paul. *When Time Shall Be No More: Prophecy Belief in Modern American Culture.* Cambridge, MA: Harvard University Press, 1992.

Cockell, Charles S. *The Meaning of Liberty Beyond Earth*. Cham: Springer, 2021.

Collins, Francis S. *The Language of God: A Scientist Presents Evidence for Belief*. New York: Free Press, 2007.

"Comprehensive Refutation of the Younger Dryas Impact Hypothesis." *Earth-Science Reviews* 223 (2021): 103888.

"Earth's Orbit." Wikipedia. Last modified 2025.

Hales, William. *A New Analysis of Chronology and Geography, History and Prophecy*. Vol. 1. London: C.J.G. & F. Rivington, 1830.

Holliday, Vance T., David J. Meltzer, David J. Kennett, et al. "Comprehensive Analysis of the Younger Dryas Impact Hypothesis." *Quaternary Science Reviews* 247 (2020): 106489.

James P. Kennett, et al. "Evidence for Deposition of 10 Million Tons of Impact Spherules Across Four Continents 12,800 y Ago." *Proceedings of the National Academy of Sciences* 106, no. 23 (2009): 10941–46.

John H. Walton. *The Lost World of Genesis One: Ancient Cosmology and the Origins Debate*. Downers Grove, IL: InterVarsity Press, 2009.

Joanna V. Morgan, et al. "The Formation of Peak Rings in Large Impact Craters." *Science* 354, no. 6314 (2016): 878–82.

Kennett, James P., Douglas J. Kennett, Allen West, et al. "Nanodiamonds in the Younger Dryas Boundary Sediment Layer." *Science* 323, no. 5910 (2009): 94–94.

Kenyon, Kathleen M. *Excavations at Jericho*. London: British School of Archaeology in Jerusalem, 1981.

Kline, Meredith G. "Space and Time in the Genesis Cosmogony." 1996. Meredith G. Kline Resource Site.

Middleton, J. Richard. *A New Heaven and a New Earth: Reclaiming Biblical Eschatology*. Grand Rapids, MI: Baker Academic, 2014.

"Milky Way." Wikipedia. Accessed 2025.

Moore, Andrew M. T., Gordon C. Hillman, and Anthony J. Legge. "Village on the Euphrates: From Foraging to Farming at Abu Hureyra." *Proceedings of the Prehistoric Society* 66 (2000): 1–40.

NASA. "Basics of Space Flight—Reference Systems." Last updated 2025. NASA Science.

NASA. "Chelyabinsk Meteor: What We Know." February 2013.

National Radio Astronomy Observatory (NRAO). "How Long Does It Take the Sun to Orbit the Center of Our Galaxy?" NRAO. Accessed 2025.

Particle Data Group. "Cosmic Microwave Background." In *Review of Particle Physics* (2024). LBL, U.S.A.

Petaev, Nicholas, S. Mukhopadhyay, A. J. S. Duarte, and R. F. L. Malley. "Large Pt Anomaly in the Greenland Ice Core Points to a Cataclysm at the Onset of Younger Dryas." *Proceedings of the National Academy of Sciences* 110, no. 32 (2013): 12917–12920.

Piat, M., et al. "Cosmic Background Dipole Measurements with the Planck." *Astronomy & Astrophysics* 571, A26 (2014).

Pope John Paul II. "Message to the Pontifical Academy of Sciences: On Evolution." October 22, 1996. Quoted in Francis S. Collins, *The Language of God: A Scientist Presents Evidence for Belief*. New York: Free Press, 2007.

Range, Molly, et al. "The Chicxulub Impact Produced a Powerful Global Tsunami." *AGU Advances* 3 (2022): 1–20.

Sarna, Nahum M. *JPS Torah Commentary: Genesis*. Philadelphia: Jewish Publication Society, 1989.

Schmidt, Klaus, and Jens Notroff. "Göbekli Tepe: A Stone Age Sanctuary in South-Eastern Anatolia." *Documenta Praehistorica* 40 (2013): 239–256.

Schulte, Peter, Laia Alegret, Ignacio Arenillas, et al. "The Chicxulub Asteroid Impact and Mass Extinction at the Cretaceous-Paleogene Boundary." *Science* 327, no. 5970 (2010): 1214–1218.

Space.com. "How Fast Is Earth Moving?" Accessed 2025.

Sutton, Matthew Avery. *American Apocalypse: A History of Modern Evangelicalism*. Cambridge, MA: Harvard University Press, 2014.

Thomas Aquinas. *Summa Theologiae* I.74.2. New Advent.

Tov, Emanuel. *Textual Criticism of the Hebrew Bible*. Minneapolis: Fortress Press, 2012.

Weber, Timothy P. *Living in the Shadow of the Second Coming: American Premillennialism, 1875–1982*. Grand Rapids, MI: Zondervan, 1979.

Woodward, S. Douglas. *Rebooting the Bible: Part 2*. Faith Happens, 2020.

Wright, N. T. *Surprised by Hope: Rethinking Heaven, the Resurrection, and the Mission of the Church*. New York: HarperOne, 2008.

Biography

C. W. Steinle is a distinguished author, teacher, and commentator recognized for his contributions to biblical theology, prophecy, and the intersection of faith and science. With a professional background as a Certified Public Accountant (CPA), Steinle brings analytical rigor to theological studies, combining research precision with pastoral insight. His bibliography spans more than twenty-five titles, including *The Rise of Western Lawlessness*—a study of cultural and ideological shifts in modern society—and *Reclaiming the Rapture*, co-authored with Dr. Douglas Hamp, which critically examines dispensationalist traditions in eschatology. Steinle's scholarship has been widely cited, with over 2,000 references on Academia.edu, and he frequently contributes to Christian media as a guest commentator and teacher.

Extensively traveled, Steinle has taught on site in Israel, Philippi, Thessaloniki, Corinth, Athens, Sinai, and Egypt, bringing historical and geographical depth to his biblical expositions. *Albatross: Faith, Science, and the Future* reflects his ongoing commitment to lifting the "albatross" of apocalyptic fear, integrating Christian faith with the intellectual and scientific horizons of the modern age.